Python Machine Learning For Beginners

Handbook For Machine Learning, Deep Learning And Neural Networks Using Python, Scikit-Learn And TensorFlow

Finn Sanders

Legal & Disclaimer

The following document is reproduced below with the goal of providing information that is as accurate and reliable as possible.

This declaration is deemed fair and valid by both the American Bar Association and the Committee of Publishers Association and is legally binding throughout the United States.

Furthermore, the transmission, duplication or reproduction of any of the following work including specific information will be considered

The information in the following pages is broadly considered to be a truthful and accurate account of facts, and as such any inattention, use or misuse of the information in question by the reader will render any resulting actions solely under their purview. There are no scenarios in which the publisher or the original author of this work can be in any fashion deemed liable for any hardship or damages that may befall them after undertaking information described herein.

Additionally, the information in the following pages is intended only for informational purposes and should thus be thought of as

Table of Contents

Introduction

The following chapters will discuss everything that you need to know in order to get started with Python machine learning. There are a lot of different things that you will be able to do when you work with traditional forms of coding. These have been used for a long time to create programs, websites, and more. But with machine learning, you are able to take all of this to a new level. Machine allows for an element of artificial intelligence, ensuring that you are going to be able to find patterns, cluster information together, and do some amazing things in the process.

Learning a new coding language used to be tricky. It could take years to master a code enough to write out some basic programs. And then add on machine learning, a process that allows a computer program to learn and do the work on its own, can take even longer. In the past, only those who had a lot of experience, and even education, could hope to do well with this part of the technological world. But with the help of this guidebook, anyone can learn how to use the Python coding language along with machine learning, and write their own programs in no time.

This guidebook is going to take some time to explore machine learning and what it is all about. We will look at some of the basics of machine learning and the difference between supervised, unsupervised, and reinforcement machine learning. We will also take a look at some of the basic libraries that you can use with this machine learning, such as Scikit-learn and TensorFlow to help you have the tools that you need. And to finish up the beginning of this guidebook, we will take a look at some of the basics of Python and how to write a few codes that you can later use with machine learning.

From here, we are going to take a look at some of the different things that you are able to do with Python machine learning. We will look at some things like K-Means clustering, support vector machines, random forests algorithms, recurrent neural networks, and even linear classifiers. All of these can be used in different situations based on what kind of program you would like to work with when you start machine learning.

There is a big world that comes with machine learning, and when you use the Python programming language to help you see results, you are going to love all of the different coding and programming tools that you want. This guidebook is going to take a look at all of the different things that you are able to work with python machine learning, so you can start working with your own projects in no time.

When you are ready to learn more about machine learning, and you want to be able to create some of your programs with the help of Python, make sure to check out this guidebook to help you get started.

Chapter 1: What is Machine Learning?

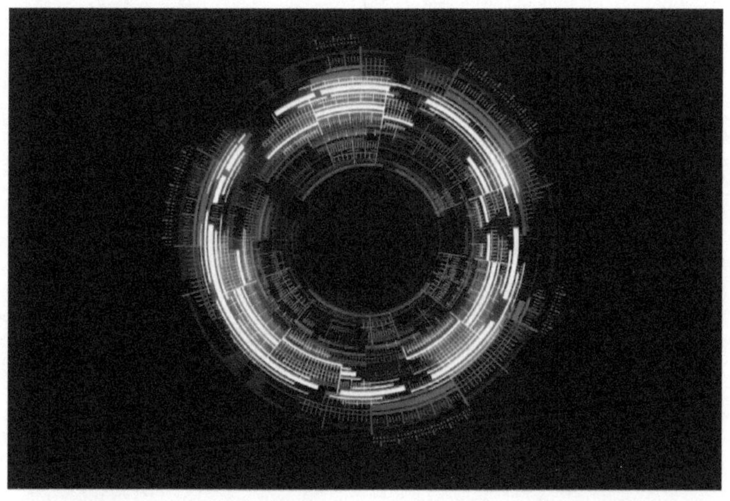

Before we start learning about some of the different parts that come with machine learning, and before we bring out some of the codes that are needed in order to be successful with machine learning, it is time to learn a bit about what machine learning is. machine learning is a type of artificial intelligence that is going to provide systems with the ability to learn from experience, without being programmed for everything that you need the process to do. Machine learning is going to be concerned with the development of computer applications that can access data and learn from it on themselves.

This kind of learning process can begin with observations or data, like instructions, examples, and direct experience to find the right patterns out of the data, and to use these predictions to know what to do in the future. The main goal that you are going to see with machine learning is that it allows the computer to learn in an automatic manner, without any help or any intervention from humans, and the computer program can make the necessary adjustments as situations change.

When you work with machine learning, you will

find that it makes analyzing large quantities of data easier than even. Machine learning can give us some results that are profitable, but of course, you first have to learn how to set it up, and there are a few resources that are needed before you are able to make this all happen. This type of coding is often going to take a bit more time to work with because you are basically training the models of machine learning to do what you want, even when you aren't there, which can really increase how much the system can do.

There are a lot of different things that you are able to use machine learning for. Any time that you aren't sure how the end result is going to turn up, or you aren't sure what the input of the other person could be, you will find that machine learning can help you get through some of these problems. If you want the computer to be able to go through a long list of options and find patterns, or find the right result, then machine learning is going to work the best for you. Some of the other things that machine learning can help out with include:

1. Voice recognition
2. Facial recognition
3. Search engines. The machine learning program is going to start learning from the answers that the individual provides, or the queries, and will start to give better answers near the top as time goes on.
4. Recommendations after shopping
5. Going through large amounts of data about finances and customers and making accurate predictions about what the company should do to increase profits and happy customers along the way.

These are just a few of the examples of when you would want to start utilizing a program that needs to be able to act on its own. Many of the traditional programs that you are going to learn how to use as a beginner are going to be much simpler than this. They will tell the computer exactly what it should do in a given situation. This works great for a lot of programs, but for things like artificial intelligence, it is not going to be enough.

With traditional coding, you will be able to figure out, or at least limit the choices, that the other person is going to give to you. And then you can add in a catch all at the end in cause the other person puts in something else. For example, if your program has the question "What is 2 + 2? You would then have a response to if they picked 4 as the answer, and then another answer to handle any other inputs that the user put into the system.

But this doesn't always work the best if you are working with some of the programs that work the best with machine learning. For example, if you are doing a search engine, you won't be able to guess each and every query that the user is going to make. If you are using voice recognition on Alexa, you won't be able to figure out each request, and how each dialect is going to sound to the machine, ahead of time. This is why machine learning can come into play and is so important.

The importance of Python

While we will take a look at Python and how it works in a bit, it is important to note that Python is one of the best languages to work with when it comes to machine learning. Python is a simple language, one that is easy enough for beginners to the world of programming to work with. Yet it still has enough power behind it to make sure that you can still get some of the intense codes done that you would like. The language has a large library, works well with other coding languages if you decide to implement them together, and it is easy enough to read, even if you don't have any kind of coding practice or experience in the past.

In this guidebook, the examples that we are going to take a look at are going to work with Python. This is going to be helpful to ensure that you are able to work on any of the codes that you would like, without having to worry about learning something that is too complicated to work with. If you have worked with Python in the past, then this is good news. And even if you have worked with a different kind of coding language in the past, this coding language is easy enough for you to learn and understand very quickly.

How to classify the machine learning algorithms

There are three main types of algorithms that all the learning algorithms of machine learning can be. These include supervised learning, unsupervised learning, and reinforced learning.

- **Supervised machine learning**

The first type of learning that we are going to take a look at is known as supervised learning. This is the kind where the human using the system is going to need to provide the input and the output that are desired, and you need to furnish the feedback to the system, based on how accurate the systems predictions are during the process of training. This basically means that the trainer needs to show a bunch of examples to the system, and shows them what is going to work and what isn't a good answer, so that the system has time to learn along the way.

After the completion of the training, the algorithm will need to apply what it learned from the data earlier on to make the best predictions. The concept that comes with supervised learning can be seen to be similar to learning under the supervision of a teacher to their students. The teacher is going to give a lesson to the students with some examples, and then the student is going to derive the new rules and knowledge from these examples. They can then take the knowledge and apply it to different situations, even if they don't match up directly to the examples that the teacher gives.

When we are looking at supervised machine learning, it is also a good thing to know the difference between the classification problems and the regression problems. A regression problem is going to be when the target will be a numeric value of some kind. But the classification is going to be a class or a tag. A regression task can help to determine the average cost of all the homes in a town, while the classification would help to determine what type of flower is in the picture based on the length of their petals.

Supervised learning is going to occur when you pick out an algorithm that is able to learn the right response to the data a user inputs to it. There are several ways that supervised machine learning can do this. It can look at examples and other targeted responses that you provide to the computer. You could include values or strings of labels to help the program learn the right way to behave.

This is a simple process to work with, but an example to look at is when a teacher is teaching their students a new topic and they will show the class examples of the situation. The students would then learn how to memorize these examples because the examples will provide general rules about the topic. Then, when they see these examples, or things that are similar, they know how to respond. However, if an example is shown that isn't similar to what the class was shown, then they know how to respond as well.

- **Unsupervised learning.**

You can also work with what is known as unsupervised learning. With these algorithms, it is not expected that you provide the output data to the computer. This is because you want the machine to figure it out based on the unknown input that the person will use there. An approach, that is known as deep learning, which can be known as an iterative approach, is going to be used to review the data and arrive at some new conclusions.

What this does is make unsupervised learning approach more suitable for use in a variety of processing tasks, which can be more complex than what you would do with supervised learning algorithms. This means that the learning algorithms that are unsupervised are going to learn just from examples, without getting any responses to it. The algorithm will strive to find the patterns that come from those examples all on its own, rather than being told the answers.

Many of the recommender types of systems that you encounter, such as when you are purchasing something online, are going to work with the help of an unsupervised learning algorithm. In this kind of case, the algorithm is going to derive what to suggest to you to purchase based on what you went through and purchased before. The algorithm then has to estimate the customers you resemble the most based on your purchases, and then will provide you with some good recommendations from there.

As we mentioned a little bit before, there are more than one type of machine learning that you can work with. Supervised learning is the first one. It is designed for you to show examples to the computer and then you teach it how to respond based on the examples that you showed. There are a lot of programs where this kind of technique is going to work well, but the idea of showing thousands of examples to your computer can seem tedious. Plus, there are many programs where this is not going t work all that well.

This is where unsupervised machine learning can come into play. We are now going to explore more of what this unsupervised machine learning is all about. Unsupervised learning is the type that will happen when your algorithm is able to learn either from mistakes or examples without having an associated response that goes with it. What this means is that with these algorithms, they will be in charge of figuring out and analyzing the data patterns based on the input that you give it.

Now, there will also be a few different types of algorithms that can work well with unsupervised machine learning. Whichever algorithm you choose to go with, it is able to take that data and restructure it so that all the data will fall into classes. This makes it much easier for you to look over that information later. Unsupervised machine learning is often the one that you will use because it can set up the computer to do most of the work without requiring a human being there and writing out all the instructions for the computer.

- **Reinforcement learning**

The third type of machine learning algorithm that you can work with is reinforcement learning. This is a type of learning that is going to occur when the algorithm is presented with examples that don't have labels, similar to what we see with unsupervised learning. However, this kind o example is going to come with some negative and positive feedback depending on the solution that is proposed by the algorithm. It is going to be associated with some applications where the algorithm is going to need to make a decision, and then these decisions will be associated with a consequence. Basically, this method is going to be similar to the trial and error method that human learning uses.

Errors are fine in this because they are going to become useful in the learning process when they are associated with a penalty such as loss of time, cost, and pain. In the process of reinforced learning, some actions are going to be more likely to succeed while others are less likely to succeed.

Machine learning processes are going to be similar to what we see with predictive modeling and data mining. In both cases, patterns are then going to be adjusted inside the program accordingly. A good example of machine learning is the recommender system. If you purchase an item online, you will then see an ad that is going to be related to that item.

There are some people who see reinforcement learning as the same thing as unsupervised learning because they are so similar, but it is important to understand that they are different. First, the input that is given to these algorithms will need to have some mechanisms for feedback. You can set these up to be either negative or positive based on the algorithm that you decide to write out.

So, whenever you decide to work with reinforcement machine learning, you are working with an option that is like trial and error. Think about when you are working with a younger child. When they do some action that you don't approve of, you will start by telling them to stop or you may put them in time out or do some other action to let them know that what they did is not fine. But, if that same child does something that you see as good, you will praise them and give them a ton of positive reinforcement. Through these steps, the child is learning what acceptable behavior is and what isn't.

To keep it simple, this is what reinforcement machine learning is going to be like. It works on the idea of trial and error and it requires that the application uses an algorithm that helps it to make decisions. It is a good one to go with any time that you are working with an algorithm that should make these decisions without any mistakes and with a good outcome. Of course, it is going to take some time for your program to learn what it should do. But you can add this into the specific code that you are writing so that your computer program leans how you want it to behave.

Understanding what deep learning is about

The next thing that we need to focus on is the idea of deep learning. This is going to be a subfield of machine learning involving algorithms that are inspired by the function and structure of the brain known as artificial neural networks. It is going to work to teach your computer to act and behave the way that a natural to humans, that is, that the system will be able to learn by example.

It is through the help of this kind of deep learning that your computer is going to be able to learn to perform the various classification tasks directly from sound, image, and text. Deep learning models are able to achieve the state of the art accuracy, which in some cases will be able to exceed the performance that you can get at the human level. Large sets of labeled data and neural network architectures are going to be used to train models with some deep learning.

As you can see, there are a lot of different parts that can come with machine learning. It is a great tool that you can use in order to get your computer or your system to do some of the things that you may struggle with. For example, machine learning can be used in order to help work with search engines, and maybe with providing you with some recommendations when you are shopping online. Even if you need to sort through a large amount of data, machine learning can come into play and help out.

The rest of this guidebook is going to spend some time looking through some of the basics that come with machine learning, and how to work with it on Python, to ensure that you are able to get the most out of this process. Let's take a closer look at some of the processes that you need to know how to work with to see amazing results with machine learning with Python.

Chapter 2: What are Deep Learning, Scikit-Learn and Tensor Flow?

Now that we know about machine learning a bit, it is time to learn a little bit more about two of the processes and libraries that are going to make the process a bit easier. You will notice that both of these are going to work well with Python, and knowing how to make the work will ensure that your

Python code is as strong and effective as possible with the machine learning that you are trying to work with.

The two processes that we are going to take a look at in this guidebook will include the Scikit-Learn and Tensor Flow. Let's take a look at how both of these can work today.

What is Scikit-Learn

We also need to take some time to learn about Scikit-learn. This is going to provide your users with a number of supervised and unsupervised learning algorithms through a consistent Python interface. We are going to take some time to learn more about Python later in this guidebook, but it is a fantastic tool that you are able to use to enhance your machine learning, and since it is for beginners, even those who have never worked with coding in the past will be able to use it.

The Scikit-learn was developed in 2007by David Cournapeau as a Google Summer of code project. This process is going to be suitable to use whether you need it commercially or academically.

Scikit-learn has been in use as a machine learning library inside of Python. It is going to come with numerous types of classification, regression, and clustering to help you get more results. Some of the algorithms that you will get to use with this system is going to include DBSCAN, k-means, random forests, support vector machines, and gradient boosting to name a few. And Scikit-learn was designed so that it would work well with some of the other popular libraries that are found on the Python code, including with SciPy and Numpy libraries.

The library itself was done all in Python, and then some of the algorithms that you are going to rely on here are going to be written with the help of Cython, in order to make sure that you get the best performance out of them as possible. You will quickly find that the Scikit-learn library is the best one for you to work with when building up some of the models of machine learning that you will need. The good news is that this library is easy to get ahold of and it is open sourced, so you can start using it when you are ready.

What is TensorFlow

Another thing that we need to take a look at here is the library that is known as TensorFlow. This is a type of framework that is going to come to us from Google and it is used when you are ready to create some of your deep learning models. This TensorFlow is going to rely on data-flow graphs for numerical computation. And it has been able to stop in and make machine learning easier than ever before.

It makes the process of acquiring the data, training some of the models of machine learning that you want to use, making predictions, and even modifying some of the future results that you see easier. Since all of these are important when it comes to machine learning, it is important to learn how to use TensorFlow.

This is a library that was developed by Google's Brain team to use on machine learning when you are doing it on a large scale. TensorFlow is going to bring together machine learning and deep learning algorithms and models and it makes them much more useful via a common metaphor. TensorFlow is going to use Python, just like what we say before, and it gives its users a front-end API that can be used when you would like to building applications, with the application being executed to a high performance C++.

TensorFlow can be used for building, training,

and running deep neural networks for image recognition, recurrent neural networks, handwritten digit classification, word embedding, and natural language processing to name a few.

Both of these libraries are going to be important when it comes to ensuring that you are on the right track with your machine learning. Both of them can also work with Python well, but the kinds of tasks that they are going to be able to handle will vary, so you need to look into that a little bit before you decide to start your project.

Chapter 3: The Basics of Python

We mentioned a bit before more about the Python language and how it can be so beneficial when you are working with machine learning. Python is one of the easiest coding languages out there, one of the best for beginners because it is so easy to learn how to use. And since it has all the power of the more advanced languages, even with it being a lot easier to use, you will find that it is perfect when it comes to learning how to work with the topic we are on.

There are a lot of different parts that come to play when you are working with the Python language. You can work with the comments, the statements, functions, and so much more. Let's get a basic look at some of the parts of the

Python code, and learn how to do a few codes, so that you are prepared to work with Python when working on this kind of code.

Comments

The first thing that we are going to take a look at here are the comments. There may be a point in your code where you would like to explain, either to yourself or to others who take a look at the code, what is going on in that point. This helps everyone to know what is really going on, or maybe it will help you to name that part of the code.

When you do this, it is going to be known as a comment. You have to put a special character in front of the comment so that the program knows that it doesn't need to read that comment, and can instead just skip over and start reading the next part of the code. For the Python language, you will need to use the # sign in front of any kind of comment that you are writing, and then the compiler will know that you don't want it to execute that point. So a good example of writing out a comment in Python would include:

```
#this is the new comment for this code
```

After you have written out the comment, and you know that it is done, you can just hit on the enter or the return button before moving on to writing more of the code on the next line. you can choose to make the comment as long or as short as you would like. And you can also write in as many of these comments as you would like in the code. However, try not to go too crazy when it comes to how many comments you are going to write out. This can make the code look messy, and can make it hard for other people to read.

Statements

Another option to work within your code is statements. Whenever you want to work on a new code, whether it is in Python or another coding language, you must add these statements inside of that code. This allows the compiler to know what you want to have happen. A statement is a unit of code that is sent over to the interpreter. Then that interpreter is able to look over the statement and execute it based on whatever command you put in.

When you are writing codes, you can choose the number of statements that will show up at one time. Sometimes there is just one statement to work with, and other times you would put in more. As long as the statements are kept inside the brackets inside the code, then it is fine to have as few or as many of them as you would like.

When you have decided that it is time to add in at least one statement to the code you are working through, you would then send it over to be taken care of by the interpreter. As long as the interpreter understands what you wrote out, it will then execute the commands. The results of your statements will show up on the computer screen. If you notice that something isn't showing up properly, then you can always go back into the code and make the necessary adjustments.

Now, this is a lot to take in and may sound confusing. Let's take a look at how you can do this:

```
x = 56
Name = John Doe
z = 10

print(x)
```

print(Name)
print(z)

When you send this over to the interpreter, the results that should show up on the screen are:

56
John Doe
10

It is as simple as that. Open up Python and give it a try to see how easy it is to just get a few things to show up in your interpreter.

Working with a variable

The next part of your code that you can spend some time with is on the variables. These variables are good to work with because they can be used to store the different parts of the code together in the right places on the computer.

This means that, if you do the process the right way, the variables are going to be found in the memory of your computer in a certain spot. Depending on the types of data that you are working on in that specific type of code, the variable is going to be there to make sure that the computer knows what space should be saved.

The first thing that we are going to do here is make sure that there is a value assigned back to the variable. If this doesn't happen, then the variable isn't going to be able to perform its job in the proper manner. If the variable is assigned a value from the start, then it will react the way that you want it to inside the code.

There are also three main types of variables that you can choose between to get the variable to work. And the one that you decide to use is going to help you figure out the type of value that you are going to assign back to it. The variables that are at your disposal to choose from will include the following:

- Float: this would include numbers like 3.14 and so on.
- String: this is going to be like a statement where you could write out something like "Thank you for visiting my page!" or another similar phrase.
- Whole number: this would be any of the other numbers that you would use that do not have a decimal point.

When you work with this particular program, remember that you won't have to go through and make a declaration in order to reserve the right amount of memory that you need. This is something that will automatically happen after you go through and add a value to the variable that you are working with. If you want to ensure that this is going to happen on its own inside the code, you just need to make sure that the equal sign is in the right place. An example of how you would be able to get this to happen would include the following:

x = 12 #this is an example of an integer assignment
pi = 3.14 #this is an example of a floating point assignment
customer name = John Doe #this is an example of a string assignment

Another thing that you can do here is to have two or more values that go to the exact same variable. There are certain instances in your code where this is going to be important. You would follow the same kind of procedure that we did above, just make sure that each part has an equal sign so they know where they are associated. So writing out something like a = b = c = 1 would be just fine in your code because each of the variables would be equal to one when you write out the code.

The keywords

When you work in Python, just like when you choose to work with some of the other coding languages that are out there, you will run across some keywords that need to be reserved as commands for the code. You must be careful about the way that these are used because they are there to tell the program how it needs to behave. You don't want to bring these out and use them in any way, or in any place, that is different than as a command, or it is going to cause some confusion with the interpreter. As we start to work on some of the machine learning codes with Python later on in this guidebook, you will start to see the keywords become more transparent as time goes on.

Coming up with the name of the identifiers

Now we need to take a look at some of the things that you need to remember when you are working with Python is that you must name all of the identifiers in the proper manner. Whenever you start to write out a new code in Python, there are going to be a few identifiers that you need to work with as well. Some of the most common ones include functions, variables, classes, and entities.

At some point, you will need to give these identifiers to get them to work the way that you would like, and to ensure that they are called up at the right time when you write the code. No matter what kind of identifier that you choose to work with, there are going to be the same rules that must be recalled to ensure that they are named the right way. Some of the rules for naming identifier includes;

- Any time that you are using letters, it is fine to use either upper case or lower case, and a combination of both is fine as well. You can also add in numbers, symbols, and an underscore to the name. any combination of these are acceptable, just make sure that there are no spaces between the characters of the name.
- Never start out the name of one of your identifiers with a number. This means that writing out a name of 4babies would result in an error on your computer. However, it is acceptable to name an identifier "fourbabies" if you would like.
- The identifier should never be one of the Python keywords and the keyword should not appear in the name at all.

Now, if you are going through and writing out

some of your own codes, and you end up not following one of these rules, the system is going to send out an error message to let you know. The error is going to show up, and then the program will automatically close out on you. This is why it is so important to be careful about the way that you name your identifiers.

When you work to pick out the identifier that you want to work with, you will want to pick out one that is easy for others, and yourself, to read through. This is going to make it easier for another programmer when they take a look through the code so that they can better understand what is going on. And going with an identifier that is descriptive is going to be helpful in terms of making sure that the code stays as organized as possible, and that it is easy for you to read through.

More about the Python language

Python is often considered by many experts in the world of coding and technology to be the best programming languages, especially if you are a beginner to this process. It is simple, it can provide you with all of the power that you need, and it is going to have enough resources and tools that you need in order to create any project that you want, including projects that have to do with machine learning. While there are other coding languages that you can work with as well, some are going to be hard to learn, and many are too difficult for those without a lot of practice and knowledge to get you started with.

One thing that you are going to like when it comes to the Python language is that it is based on the English language, which means that picking up on this language is going to be easier because you don't have to deal with a lot of words you can't even read. And despite the fact that it is designed so that beginners are able to get the most out of it, there is going to be a ton of power behind any of the codes that you work on there.

As someone who is just getting started in Python, you are also going to enjoy the library that is available with this coding language. And this library is going to make it a lot easier for you to write out some of the codes that you need for any kind of program.

As a beginner, you may also like that there is a fairly large community that comes with this language. Because this language is used by so many people all throughout the world, there are lots of resources that you can work with to see the best results. You can find communities and forums online that can help to answer some of your questions, and who will ensure that you get your program done and running, even if you need a little help.

Making sure Python is on your computer

Now, if you are ready to start coding and you have decided that Python is the option for you, then there are a few things that you may want to consider having nearby to help make this process a bit easier. First, it is a good idea to check that you have a strong text editor already in place on your computer. This is the specific software that you will use to write out your codes in Python. It doesn't have to be complicated, Notepad on a Windows computer words just fine, but you need to make sure it is in place.

Once you have checked to see if the text editor is in place, it is time to download the Python program so you can start writing out the codes. Python is a free programming language so you won't have to worry about paying high fees or anything with it. The IDE, or the environment that runs the codes, is free for users as well.

To get this coding program set up, you just need to go to the Python website and then click on the version that you are interested in using. There are several options available based on what has just been released, what features you want, and what operating system is on your computer.

While downloading the Python programming language, you must make sure that you are also downloading the IDE at this time. The IDE is the basic environment that you will work on when writing your codes. This IDE will also hold onto the compiler that is needed to help interpret all the codes you write. You can choose to go with the IDE that comes automatically with Python. This one is designed to specifically work with Python. With that said, there are other options of

IDEs that may have some special features you would enjoy working with.

As you can see, the Python language is not as complicated to work with as it may seem. You will be able to enjoy the benefits of using it right away, once your environment and IDE is in place so that you can actually write out the codes that you need to use. Make sure to review some of the topics about Python that we have learned about in this chapter, and learn a bit about the language so that you are ready to progress through this guidebook and do some amazing things with the machine learning we will talk about.

Chapter 4: Setting Up Your Environment

Now that we know a little bit more about machine learning and we have learned some about the Python coding language, it is time to get your environment all set up. This is an important step to take before you try to work more with machine learning and deep learning. And to help you set up this great environment, you need to make sure that your two libraries, the TensorFlow and the Scikit-Learn are all set up and ready to go.

Installing Scikit-Learn

The first library that we are going to important and get all set up is going to be the Scikit-learn. This is a library that is supported on Python 2.7 and above so if you have one of those already installed on your computer, then you are ready to go. But before you go through and install this library, ensure that you already have the SciPy and Numpy libraries installed as well. If those are not present, then go through and install them and then install the Scikit-Learn.

The installation of all of these important libraries can be done with the help of pip. This is a type of tool that comes with Python, which means that if you have already installed Python on your system, or once you are done with the installation, then you will get pip. From here, you will be able to use the following command in order to get the scikit-learn ready to go:

pip install scikit-learn

From here the installation will be able to run and then it will complete once all of that is done. It is also possible for you to go through and use the option of conda to help install this library. The command that you will want to use to make sure that this happens is:

```
conda install scikit-learn
```

Once you notice that the installation of scikit-learn is complete, it is time to do some importation to get it over to the Python program. This step is necessary in order to use the algorithms that come with it. The good news is that the command to make this happen is going to be done. You simply need to go to your command line and type in import sklearn.

If your command is able to go through without leaving behind an error message, then you know that the installation that you just did was successful. After you are done with all of these steps, your scikit-learn library is on the computer, it is compatible with the Python program, and it is going to be ready to use.

How to install TensorFlow

The next thing that we need to take a look at when it comes to downloading and installing your environment is the TensorFlow library. This TensorFlow is going to come with some APIs for programming languages including Rust, Java, Go, Haskell, and C++. We are going to take a look here at installing this kind of library on a Windows computer. When you are on Windows, you can download this library with Anaconda or pip.

The native pip is going to be able to take TensorFlow and install it on your system, without having to go through and place it on a virtual environment. But one thing that you need to note here is that installing the TensorFlow with a pip can end up interfering with the other installations of Python that you may have on your system.

The good news here is that the only think you will need to run to make this work is a single command, and once that command is in place, TensorFlow is going to be installed and ready to use on your system. And when this library is installed with the help of a pip, the user is going to be given the option to run this program from any kind of directory that they want on their computer.

To go through and install this library with the help of Anaconda, you need to first go through and create an environment that is virtual. However, when you are taking a look at Anaconda on its own, you will see that it is recommended that you will install this library with the help of the pip install, rather than working with the command for the conda install.

Before you get started here, make sure that you

are working with Python 3.5 or above on the Windows system. Python 3 is a nice one because it is already going to have the pip 3 program in place, which can often be used for the installation of TensorFlow. This means that you will be able to use the command for pip3 install to make everything work the way that you would like. If you are interested in getting the CPU only version for this library, you can use the command of:

pip3 install – upgrade tensorflow

if you would like to make sure that you are installing the GPU version of the Tensorflow program, you would need to go through and use the following command to make it happen:

pip3 install – upgrade tensorflow-gpu

This is going to ensure that you are able to install

TensorFlow on the Windows system that you are using. But another option that you can use to install this library so that you can use it with Python and all of your other machine learning algorithms will include being able to install it with the help of the Anaconda package.

Pip is a program that is automatically going to get installed when you get Python on your system. But the Anaconda program isn't. this means that if you would like to make sure that TensorFlow is able to get installed with the use of the Anaconda program, you first need to take the time to install this program. To do this, visit the website for Anaconda, download it from the website, and then find the instructions for installation from that same site.

Once you have gone through and installed the Anaconda program, you should notice that it comes with a package that is called conda. This is a good package to take some time to look at and explore a bit because it will work when you want to manage any installation packages or manage virtual environments. To get some access to this package, you just need to start up the Anaconda program.

From here, you can go to your Windows main screen, click on Start, and then choose All Programs. You will need to expand things out in order to expand and see Anaconda and look at the folder. You can then click on the Anaconda prompt. This is going to launch the anaconda prompt on your system. If you need to see the details of this particular package, you would just need to run the command "conda info". This will allow you to see more details about the package and the package manager.

There is something else that is really unique when it comes to Anaconda, and that you may want to learn a bit about so that you can help with machine learning. It helps us to create a virtual Python environment of your own with the help of the conda package. This virtual environment is going to be an isolated copy of Python, with the capability of maintaining all of the files that it needs, all of the paths, and all of the directories. This is a great thing because it is going to allow you to do all of this and work with a specific version of Python, or any of the other libraries that you want, without having a negative effects on the other projects that you are working on.

These virtual environments are going to be great because they will provide the user with a way of isolating projects and you can then avoid problems that may arise as a result of version requirements and different dependencies through different components. Note that this is an environment that is different from the normal python environment that you already downloaded. This is important because it ensures that the virtual environment is not going to be able to have any effect, whether good or bad, with some of the normal projects that you do with Python.

At this point, we are going to work to create a virtual environment for the TensorFlow package. This can be done with the help of the conda create command. Since we are going to create an environment that is known as tensorenviron, you would use the syntax that is below:

conda create -n tensorenviron

At this point, the program is going to ask you whether or not you would like to allow the process of creating the environment to continue on, or if you would like to cancel the work that you are doing. You will want to type in the “y” and then hit the enter key to move on. This will allow the installation to continue on successfully to see the results that you want.

After you have gone through and created this kind of environment, you will need to take some time to activate it. Without the right activation, you won't be able to use this new environment that you have set up. The activation is going to be done with the help of the activate command. And then you will list out the name of the environment that you want to work with. An example of how you would pull up the environment that you just created includes:

Activate tensorenviron

Now that you have been able to activate the TensorFlow environment, it is time to go ahead and make sure that the package for TensorFlow are going to be installed too. You are able to do this by using the command below:

Conda install tensorflow

From here, the computer is going to present you with a list of all of the different packages that you can install together along with the package for TensorFlow if you would like. You will be prompted to decide if you would like to install these packages or not. You can then type in the "y" and hit the enter key on the keyboard.

Once you agree to doing this, the installation of this package is going to get started right away. However, notice that this particular process for installation is going to take a bit of time, so you need to wait it out and remain patient. However, the speed that your connection for internet goes is going to determine the amount of time that the installation process is going to take. The progress and how far the installation has gone and has yet to go is going to be shown on a prompt window.

After some time, the installation process will be complete, and you can then take some time to determine if the installation process was successful or not. This is pretty easy to do because you just need to run the import statement with Python. The statement is going to be done from the regular terminal of Python. If you are doing this with the Anaconda prompt, you can just type in "python" and hit the enter key. This is going to make sure that you end up in the terminal for Python and from there, you can run the import statement below:

Import tensorlow as tf

If you find that the package wasn't installed in the proper manner, you are going to end up with an error message on the screen after you do this code. If you don't see an error message, then you know that the installation of the package was successful.

Chapter 5: Getting Started with Scikit-Learn

If you are a programmer who wants to work more with Python, or you are interested in learning more about machine learning with Python, then you definitely need to spend some more time learning about Scikit-Learn and how it all works. This kind of program was developed in the summer of 2007. Later, Matthieu Brucher joined the team and started to use the work of David Cournapeau as a part of his own thesis work. Then in 2010, the INRIA got involved and the first public release of this was made available to others to use in January 2010.

This project has really grown to new proportions over time. it now has more than 30 active contributors, and there are even some paid sponsorships from the Python Software

Foundation, Tinyclues, Google, and INRIA to ensure that it can continue to be developed, even though many of the users will not have to pay anything to make this happen.

But this brings up the question of what this library is all about. Scikit-learn is going to provide you with a ton of unsupervised and supervised learning algorithms that you can rely on via a consistent interface with Python. This means that it allows you to do a lot of the work that you want with machine learning with the help of Python.

This library is licensed under a permissive simplified BSD license, and then many Linux distributions have been able to use it, encouraging it to be used and grow through commercial and academic use. This particular library is going to be build upon the Scientific Python, or the SciPy library, that you need to have installed on your system before you can even use the scikit-learn. The stack that is found in this, and which is going to be really helpful when you are working with machine learning includes:

1. Pandas: These are important because it includes the data structure and the analysis that you need.
2. Sympy: This is going to be the symbolic mathematics
3. iPython: This is going to be an enhanced interactive kind of console
4. Matplotlib: This is a good tool to have because it comes with a comprehensive 2D and 3D plotting.
5. SciyPY: This is going to be a fundamental library that can be used for scientific computing
6. NumPy: This is going to be the base n-dimensional array package.

The modules and the Extensions that come with SciPy are going to be known as SciKits. This is why the modules that help to provide us with the learning algorithms that we need are going to be known as scikit-learn.

The vision that comes with this kind of library is going to include a higher level of support and robustness. This is a good thing because both of these need higher levels to make sure that the production system is going to work the way that we want. In the process, there needs to be a deeper focus on concerns such as performance, documentation, collaboration, code quality, and ease of use.

What are the features

When you are working with this library, you may be curious what it is all about, and why it is such a good option for you to work with to help you with machine learning. The Scikit-Learn library is going to be focused with modeling data. It won't take the time to look at summarizing data, manipulating data, and loading data. If you want to do any of those three things, you would want to work with the Pandas or the NumPy libraries. Some of the different groups of models that you can get through the scikit-learn library will include:

1. Supervised models: This library is able to provide you with a lot of different generalized linear models for your needs. This would include things like decision trees, support vector machines, neural networks, lazy methods, naïve bayes, discriminate analysis, and more.
2. Manifold learning: These can be used in order to depict and even to summarize multi-dimensional data that may seem a bit complex.
3. Parameter tuning: This is going to be a

tool that will help you to get the most out of your supervised models.

4. Feature selection: This part of the library is going to help you see and identify meaningful attributes from which to create a new supervised model.
5. Feature extraction: This is going to be used in order to define the attributes to the image and the text data.
6. Ensemble methods: This one is going to be helpful when you want to combine the predictions that a few different supervised models are going to come up with on their own.
7. Dimensionality reduction: This method is going to be helpful when it comes to reducing the number of attributes that are needed in data for summarization, feature selection, and visualization. One example of this is going to be the principal component analysis.

8. Datasets: This is going to be where you can test out the datasets that you have, the ones that are for generating datasets with specific properties for investigating model behavior.
9. Cross validation: This one is going to be helpful when you want to estimate how well the supervised model you have is going to perform on data that is unseen.
10. Clustering: This is where you are able to group any of the unlabeled data, such as the K-means that we will talk about a bit later.

As you can see, there are a lot of different types of things that you are able to use with the scikit-learn library. This is why it is so important for you to learn about this library, and figure out how to get it to work the best for you.

Chapter 6: K-Nearest Neighbors Algorithm

One of the algorithms that we are going to focus on is the K-Nearest Neighbors Algorithm, or KNN. This is a type of supervised machine learning so we get some time to look at how this works as well. When you work with the KNN algorithm, you are going to use it to search through the data that you have for k most similar examples of any kind of instance that you are trying to work with. Once you are able to do this and see some success, then the KNN algorithm will move on to look through all of the information that you have and will summarize it. Then the algorithm will use the results that you receive in order to make some predictions for that instance.

Any time that you bring out the KNN algorithm

model, you will find that your learning is going to become more competitive. The reason that this is going to work because there is some competition between the different parts, or the different elements, in various models so that you get the best predictions based on the data on hand.

The KNN algorithm is going to work a bit different than a few of the other algorithms that we are going to discuss in this guidebook. In some instances, it is seen as a lazier approach to learning, mainly because it isn't going to create any of the models that you need, until you go in and ask it for a new predictions. Depending on the situation you are working with, this can be a good thing because waiting to make new predictions ensures that the data you have at hand, and the data you are using for these predictions is always relevant for the tasks that you want.

If the program went through and just tries to do predictions on regular intervals, or each time that you put in new data, this can be helpful in some situations. But if you want to see what happens in certain situations, or you want to just look at a certain customer group, having this happen all the time, or update with all the information rather than just the information that you want, will make you miss out on things. The KNN algorithm can help out with this.

There are a lot of benefits that come when you decide to work with the KNN algorithm. When you are working with this, you are able to cut through some of the noise that comes with your data set. This noise can be really loud if you have a lot of data to go through, and getting rid of some of that noise can make a big difference in the information that you are able to get. And if you are trying to handle and go through larger amounts of data all at once, then this is the algorithm that you should choose. Unlike some of the others that are going to be more limited on the amount of data they can sort through, the KNN algorithm doesn't have this kind of issue, and you are able to use it on large and small data sets.

One of the biggest issues that can come when you use this algorithm is that the computational costs are going to be higher. This is especially true when you compare it to some of the other algorithms that are available to do the same thing. The reason that the computational costs are going to be higher is because this algorithm is going to look through each and every data point, rather than clustering them, and then it can send you a good prediction to look over and make decisions from.

When do we work with the KNN algorithm?

You can use this algorithm for both regression and classification problems of prediction, which can make it really powerful and useful. With that said, it is going to be used the most with classification problems in your industry. There are three important things that you need to consider when you want to evaluate the technique and these include:

1. How easy it is to interpret the output that you have.
2. The calculation of time.
3. Predictive power.

When the KNN algorithm is compared to some of the other algorithms, including random forests, CART, and logistic regression, you will see that it can fair well across all of the parameters and considerations. Often this algorithm is going to be used because it is easy to interpret the results that it provides, and the calculation is going to be lower.

How does this algorithm work?

There are a few steps that you are able to follow when it comes to using the KNN algorithm. Some of these steps include:

1. Load the data into the algorithm for it to read through.
2. Initialize the value that you are going to use and rely on for k.
3. When you are ready to get the predicted class, iteration from one to total number of the data points that you use for training, you can use the following steps to help.
    a. Start by calculating the distance

that is in between each of your test data, and each row of your training data. We are going to work with the Euclidean distance as our metric for distance since it's the most popular method. Some of the other metrics that you may choose to work with here include the cosine and Chebyshev.

b. Sort the calculated distances going in ascending order, based on their distance values.
c. Get the k rows from the sorted array.
d. Get the most frequent class for these rows.
e. Return back the class prediction.

Why is KNN non-parametric?

When we take a look at non-parametric, it means

that we are not making any assumptions of the way that the distribution of the underlying data is done. Non-parametric methods don't need to have a fixed number of parameters in the model. In a similar manner, when you work with KNN, the model parameters will actually grow with the training data set. A good way to imagine that each training case is going to be more of a parameter of the model, and that is how this algorithm works.

What is the difference between K-mean and KNN

In the next chapter, we are going to talk about K-means, and it is going to be a big confusing for those who are working with machine learning for the first time. Many times it is easy to get confused and you may not know what the difference is between these two statistical techniques. Some of the differences that you are going to start to notice when you get started with these two, and you gain some more experience with them will include:

1. K-means is going to be a technique that you use with unsupervised learning. This means that there isn't going to be any dependent variables present. On the other hand, the KNN is going to be an algorithm for supervised learning. This means that there is going to be a dependent variable that exists.
2. K-means is going to be a good clustering technique which is going to try and split the data points out into K-clusters such that the points in each cluster will tend to be near each other. But with the K-nearest neighbor, you are going to try and find the classification of the point, and then it is going to combine together the classification of the K nearest points from

that.

Why should I use KNN?

There are a lot of different algorithms that you can use when it comes to the KNN algorithm. So, why would you want to choose to go with this algorithm over some of the others that are available for you to choose? Some of the benefits that come with KNN include:

1. It can work well with problems, even if they are considered multi-class.
2. You are able to apply this algorithm to both problems that are regressive and those that are classification.
3. There aren't any assumptions that come up with the data. This ensures that you get the information that you want, rather than having any assumptions in the place causing some issues.

4. It is an easy algorithm to work with. It is easy to understand, especially if you are brand new to the machine learning process.

However, there are more options of algorithms that you are able to work with because the KNN algorithm isn't going to be perfect in each and every situation that you go to. Some of the negatives that come with using the KNN algorithm includes:

1. It is going to be computationally and memory intensive expensive. If you don't have the right system and the right amount of space to work with the, it is going to make it more difficult to see the results that you want from this algorithm.
2. If there are a lot of independent variables that you are going to work with, you will find that the KNN algorithm is going to

struggle.

3. The KNN algorithm isn't going to work that well if you have any rare event, or skewed, target variables.
4. Sensitive to scale of data.

For any given problem that you have, a small value of k is going to lead to a larger amount of variance in the predictions that you will get. In addition, when you set the k to a bigger value, there could be some issues with a large model bias along the way.

At some point, you may need to go through and create some dummy variables in order to figure out some of the categorical variables with this algorithm. This is going to be something that you do instead of original categorical variables. Unlike what you would do with a regression, you can work with creating these k dummies rather than the (k-1). For example, you could have a categorical variable that is known as Department, and inside this, there are going to be five categories or levels that are unique. Because of this, each of the dummy variables has 1 against its department and else 0.

How to find the best K value?

A good way to figure out the most optimal value of K is to do some cross-validation. It is going to be important to use this cross-validation in order to estimate the validation error. To do this, you will hold out a subset of the training set from the model building process.

Cross-validation (let's say that it is 10 fold validation), will involve you going through and randomly dividing up the training set into 10 groups, which are also known as folds, while trying to keep them close to equal in size. From that, 90 percent of the data is going to be used to train the model of your choice, and then the rest of the ten percent is going to be used in order to validate the model that you use.

The misclassification rate that you are going to need to work with is going to be computed using that ten percent that you saved back for the validation data. This procedure is going to need to go through and repeat itself ten different times. Each of the different groups of observations that you run into are going to be treated as a validation set each of the ten times that you go through with it. It is going to be a result to 10 estimates of the validation error, which are then going to be averaged out.

Chapter 7: What is K-Means Clustering?

The next item on the list to discuss is the idea of k-means clustering. This is a pretty basic idea when it comes to machine learning, and it is going to do some to machine learning, but it is going to go a long way to helping you see some results with your programming. The basic idea with this is that you can take a lot of the data in your system that hasn't been labeled, and then put them together in a group of their own clusters.

Clustering is going to fall under the category of an algorithm that is unsupervised machine learning. It is going to be applied when the data that you have doesn't come with any labels on it. The goal of this kind of algorithm is to ensure that you are able to identify the groups or the clusters that are found inside your data.

The idea of working with these clusters is that the objects that end up in the same cluster are going to be very closely related to one another, and have fewer similarities to the items that are in some of the other clusters. The similarity here is going to be a metric that can reflect the strength of the relationship between these two objects of data.

You may find that this clustering is going to be applied highly in the use of data mining, especially if it is exploratory. It could also have uses in other kinds of fields including computer graphics, bio-informatics, data compression, image analysis, information retrieval, machine learning, and pattern recognition.

The algorithm is going to form some clusters of data that is based on how similar the data values are. You are then required to specify the value of

K, which are the number of clusters that you expect the algorithm to make out of the data. The algorithm will start out by selecting a centroid value for each of these clusters. And then it is going to go through three steps in an iterative manner includes:

1. You will want to start with the Euclidian distance between each data instance and the centroids for all of the clusters.
2. Assign the instances of data to the cluster of centroid with the nearest distance possible.
3. Calculate the new centroid values, depending on what the mean values of the coordinates of the data instances from the corresponding cluster.

How to work with k-means clustering?

For this, the input that you use for the k-means is just going to be found in matrix X. for the most part, you will be able to add in some kind of organization of your choice to ensure that each of the rows you create will be a different sample, while each of the columns are going to include a different kind of feature or factor. To make this happen, there are going to be two main steps that you must follow to get the k-means algorithm.

For the first step, it is time to choose the centers that you want to use for these clusters. If you are not sure about which centers are going to work the best for you, it is fine if you just go with a random point and use that as your center for this time. if it seems a little bit off after some time, you can go back through and make changes later.

The second step is going to be with the main loop. After you have your centers chosen, it is time for you to decide which cluster each of your points will belong to. You can look at all of the samples that you have and then choose the center of the cluster that fits into it the best.

From here, you will be able to spend some time re-calculating the cluster centers. In this part, you are going to do this based on the center points that you assigned to each part. This is pretty simple because it is done when you take all of your samples and then figure out what the mean of those samples are. And once you are able to come up with an answer to this, you will have the k-mean.

You are going to continue to do this until you get the algorithm to converge. There are no more changes in the cluster centers or assignments. For the most part, this will happen in five steps or less. You should notice that this is going to be very different from the gradient descent that you will see in deep learning, which could end up with many iterations before they end up with a convergence.

To understand what is going on, let's take a look at how the k-means is going to work.

```
---- -^-
|1|  |2|
---  ---
|  |
|  |
|  |
-*- ---
|3| |4|
--- ---
```

This is going to be our initialization point. Here we will have four vectors that are going to be labeled as 1, 2, 3, and 4. The two cluster centers, which are k=2, have been randomly assigned in this one to points 2 and 3. We used the (*) and the (^) signs to help denote these. It is now time to begin with the main loop.

The first step that we need to do is decide which cluster each of our points is going to belong to. We are going to see that the points 1 and 3 are going to be the cluster center on the left, because they are both closer to that one than the center cluster. And then the points 2 and 4 will be in the center cluster on the right because they fit closer to that one.

The second step is to do a recalculation of the cluster centers based on the points that will belong with that cluster. The (*) cluster is going to move in between 1 and 3 because this ends up being the main of those too points. The same thing is going to happen with the (^) cluster but it will move between 2 and 4 since this will be the mean of these 2 points. It is pretty easy to come up with the mean for these two points because of the lower amount of data points, but with more complex data, you would be able to use an algorithm to make it happen. For this example, you would need to uses the following code:

You will not see any changes happen in the subsequent iterations so for this example, we are going to be all done.

The difference between fuzzy and soft k-means

As you are working on these, you may notice that when you are working with the k-means, they are going to be really sensitive as you move them, especially to what is known as the initialization. But how do we fix this so that the areas aren't so sensitive, and you will be able to get some accurate answers that you are actually able to work on?

One strategy that you can use in machine learning is to restart the k-means two or three times. Then you can use the result that seems to give you the best final cost in the end. In the next section, we will take some time to break down this process so you are able to get it to work well with you. But what this is letting us know is that the cost function is going to be susceptible to the local minima, and you can mess around with it a bit to get the answers that you are looking for.

You may find that one of the methods that can help you to get through this challenge and see some results is to add in what is known as a membership that is fuzzy to each class you have. These fuzzy points mean that each of the data points aren't really going to belong to one class or another. But, the points are going to be an amount of the membership as a whole instead.

For example, you may have a fuzzy point that fits in to 60 percent of the first cluster, and then it will also match up to 40 percent of the second cluster. You can then use this to get the soft k-means by making a few small adjustments to the algorithm that you used before. The first part is going to be the same, you just need to make sure that the first k-cluster centers back to the random points that are in your set of data. But the changes that you see are going to come on the inside of some of your main loops.

So the first step that we will need to do is to calculate the cluster responsibilities. The formula we will use is the following:

r(kn) = exp[-b * d(m(k), x(n))] / sum[j=1..K] { exp[-b * d(m(j), x(n))] }

From here, you can see that the r(k,n) is going to work out as a fraction, some number that is in between 0 and 1, where you can interpret the hard k-means or the regular k-means to be the case where r(k,n) is always exactly equal to 0 or 1. The d(*,*) can be any valid distance metric, but the Euclidean or squared Euclidean distances are the ones that are used the most.

Then for the second step, we are going to work on a formula that is similar to the hard k-means, but we are just recalculating the means based on the responsibilities that we want to sent with it. The algorithm that we are going to use for this includes:

m(k) = sum[n=1..N] { r(k,n)* x(n)] / sum[n-1..N] { r(k,n) }

So, when you take the time to look at this algorithm above, you are going to see that it is similar to the weighted mean. This is going to show you that if the r(k,n) is higher, then the mean is going to be more important to the cluster of k. When you see this, it is going to show that this is going to have the biggest influence on the calculation of the mean. But if the mean is higher when you look at the algorithm, you will know that the opposite is true.

What is the k-means objective function?

Just like what we spent some time talking about with supervised learning before, you must make sure that you spend some of your time looking at and talking about the objective function that you wish to get the most out of with your unsupervised learning. To get started with this idea, we will need to use what is known as the

Euclidean distance to make it easier to measure the distance of each center. The function that we will need to use to figure this out includes:

J = sum[n=1..N] {sum[k=1..K] { r(k,n) || m(k) = x(n) ||^2} }

This is simply the squared distance that has been weighted by the responsibilities. So if the x(n) part is far away from the mean of your k cluster, hopefully the responsibility of that one is set to be pretty low. What we have done here is known as a coordinate descent. It means that we are trying to move in the direction of a smaller J with respect to just one of the variables at a time. You can see that this is true because we are only updated one of the variables at a time.

When you look at this, you will notice that there is going to be a little guarantee mathematically that all of the iterations will result in the objective function that you work with decreasing. What this means is that, if you do this enough, and you do it in the right manner, you will find that over time these are going to converge. However, just because there is a convergence doesn't mean that they reach the global minimum that you want. The numbers will go off the patterns that are there, and they will look more at the math, rather than being worried about what is the most important to you.

Adding in the soft k-means to the code you are writing.

Now that we have taken some time to look at the idea of what the k-means is all about, and some of the different ways that it is able to help you create the solution that you need in your program, it is time to implement the ideas that we have talked about using python and the other skills of machine learning to make this work.

And we can do this by implementing the soft k-means into the code.

To make this happen, you want to make sure that you are going with the standard imports, and have them work with the utility functions. This is basically going to be the same thing at the Euclidean distance, and the cost function together. The formula that you will be able to use to make this happen includes:

```
import numpy as np
import matplotlib.pyplot as plt

def d(u, v):
    diff = u - v
    return diff.dot(diff)

def cost(X, R, M):
    cost = 0
    for k in xrange(len(M)):
```

```
    for n in xrange(len(X)):
        cost += R[n,k]*d(M[k], X[n])
  return cost
```

After this part, we are going to take the time to define your function so that it is able to run the k-means algorithm before plotting the result. This is going to end up with a scatterplot where the color will represent how much of the membership is inside of a particular cluster. We would do that with the following code.

```
def plot_k_means(X, K, max_iter=20,
beta=1.0):
  N, D = X.shape
  M = np.zeros((K, D))
  R = np.ones((N, K)) / K

  # initialize M to random
  for k in xrange(K):
    M[k] = X[np.random.choice(N)]
```

```
grid_width = 5
grid_height = max_iter / grid_width
random_colors = np.random.random((K, 3))
plt.figure()

costs = np.zeros(max_iter)
for i in xrange(max_iter):
    # moved the plot inside the for loop
    colors = R.dot(random_colors)
    plt.subplot(grid_width, grid_height, i+1)
    plt.scatter(X[:,0], X[:,1], c=colors)
    # step 1: determine assignments /
resposibilities
    # is this inefficient?
    for k in xrange(K):
        for n in xrange(N):
            R[n,k] = np.exp(-beta*d(M[k], X[n])) /
np.sum( np.exp(-beta*d(M[j], X[n])) for j in
xrange(K) )

    # step 2: recalculate means
```

```
    for k in xrange(K):
        M[k] = R[:,k].dot(X) / R[:,k].sum()

    costs[i] = cost(X, R, M)
    if i > 0:
        if np.abs(costs[i] - costs[i-1]) < 10e-5:
            break

plt.show()
```

Notice here that both the M and the R are going to be matrices. The R is going to become the matrix because it holds onto 2 indices, the k and the n. M is also a matrix, because it is going to contain the K individual D-dimensional vectors. The beta variable is going to control how fuzzy or spread out the cluster memberships are and will be known as the hyperparameter. From here, we are going to create a main function that will create random clusters and then call up the functions that we have already defined above.

```
def main():
    # assume 3 means
    D = 2 # so we can visualize it more easily
    s = 4 # separation so we can control how far apart the means are
    mu1 = np.array([0, 0])
    mu2 = np.array([s, s])
    mu3 = np.array([0, s])

    N = 900 # number of samples
    X = np.zeros((N, D))
    X[:300, :] = np.random.randn(300, D) + mu1
    X[300:600, :] = np.random.randn(300, D) + mu2
    X[600:, :] = np.random.randn(300, D) + mu3

    # what does it look like without clustering?
    plt.scatter(X[:,0], X[:,1])
    plt.show()
    K = 3 # luckily, we already know this
    plot_k_means(X, K)
```

```
    # K = 5 # what happens if we choose a "bad" K?
    # plot_k_means(X, K, max_iter=30)

    # K = 5 # what happens if we change beta?
    # plot_k_means(X, K, max_iter=30, beta=0.3)


if __name__ == '__main__':
    main()
```

Now that we have gone through some of the formulas that you can use with the k-means and we understand how these work and why they are so important, take some time to open up your python compiler and give it a try. You will find that these are able to help you see some great results with your work, gather and analyze the clusters, and get a better understanding the information that you have right in front of you.

Chapter 8: What are Support Vector Machines?

Now that we have taken some time to look at a few of the methods that you will need to know about machine learning, it is time to come and learn a bit about a process that is known as SVM, or support vector machine. The SVM is going to be something that a programmer is able to use for many challenges that they face with regression and with classification that can come up during your work. With this one, a lot of the work that has to be done on the problems of classification can make the work that you are doing can be really tricky. But the SVM algorithm is a way to ensure that you are able to handle all of the challenges that do occur.

When you are ready to do some work with SVM

in machine learning, you will need to take each of the data set items that you have, and then plot them in a way so that they become just one point on an n-dimensional space. N is going to be the amount of features that you plan to use with this. Then you can take the value of all the features and work to translate this over to the value that shows up on your coordinates. The job that you can do when you reach this point is to determine the hyperplane because this is the part that will show you the difference between the various classes that show up.

Here you will notice that with the SVM algorithm, there are going to be a few support vectors that can often show up. But many of these are going to just be the coordinates of individual observations that you see. Then you can use the SVM to be the frontier that will separate them out to classes, and there are going to be two that you should focus on, the line and the hyperplane.

To this point, a lot of what we are saying here is going to seem confusing and may not make all that much sense. And you may not know why you would want to even learn about and use this SVM idea in the first place. But there are some steps that you can take to really find how this sorts out the data that you have.

First, you will need to take some time to look at the hyperplane. As you go through you may find that there are a few of these hyperplanes that you can pick from. And there is the added challenge hat you want to make sure that out of those options, you go with the one that is the best for all of your needs. The good news is that even if you have a few options, there are some easy steps that you can use in order to pick the right one. These steps include:

- We are going to start out with three hyperplanes that we will call 1, 2, and 3. Then we are going to spend time figuring out which hyperplane is right so that we can classify the star and the circle.

- The good news is there is a pretty simple rule that you can follow so that it becomes easier to identify which hyperplane is the right one. The hyperplane that you want to go with will be the one that segregates your classes the best.

- That one was easy to work with, but in the next one, our hyperplanes of 1, 2, and 3 are all going through the classes and they segregate them in a manner that is similar. For example, all of the lines or these hyperplanes are going to run parallel with each other. From here you may find that it is hard to pick which hyperplane is the right one.

- For the issue that is above, we will need to use what is known as the margin. This is basically the distance that occurs between the hyperplane and the nearest data point from either of the two classes. Then you will be able to get some numbers that can help you out. These numbers may be closer together, but they will point out which hyperplane is going to be the best.

The example that we talked about above is only one of the times that you will find SVM as a helpful tool with machine learning. When you are looking through some of the data points that are available, and you see that there is a good margin that points out the separation, then the SV method is going to be a great option to use to get the work done. In addition, the effectiveness that you are able to get form this kind of model will end up with an increase any time that you have a project with dimensional spaces that are higher than normal.

You may not use the SVM method all of the time. But even so, working with this particular technique is going to help you to use a subset of training points that come with a decision function, or the support vector, and when the memory of the program you are working on is high enough to allow you to do this.

While there are benefits that you will get with this method depending on the project that you are working on, there are still going to be some times when the SVM method is not the best for you. When you work with a data set that is large, the SVM may not provide you with options that are the most accurate. The training time with these larger sets of data can be high, and this will disappoint you if you need to get through the information quickly. And if there are some target classes that are overlapping, the SVM is going to behave in a way that is different than what you want.

Chapter 9: Bringing it Back to Scikit-Learn with Neural Networks

The next thing that you would want to take a look at when it comes to machine learning is known as neural networks. These are going to be another method of unsupervised machine learning. These networks are often used in machine learning can be used a lot because they are going to help you to catch on to the patterns that are present. This is done at different levels, and in a way that is faster and more effective than you can do with the human eye.

In the neural networks, each of the layers that are gone through will spend time there to see if there is a pattern that is found in the image that it looks at. If the network isn't able to find a brand new pattern when they go to a new layer, then it is going to go through a process that is meant to help it start the next layer. This process is going to go on and on, with one layer on top of the other, until all of the layers for this neural network algorithm are created, and the program is able to give a good prediction back about what is found inside the image you had it scan.

There are a few things that will happen at this point, based on how the program works. If the algorithm went through the process above, and was able to sort through all of the different layers, it will then make a prediction. If that prediction is right, the neurons in the system will turn out stronger than ever. This is because the program has used artificial intelligence in order to make some strong associations between the patterns and the object. The more times that the system can come back with the right answer, the more efficient it will be when you turn it on and use it again.

Now, this may seem a little bit farfetched and like it isn't something that could actually happen. But a closer examination of these neural networks will help us to see how they work together and why they are so important. For our example, let's say that your goal is to create a program that is able to take a picture that you input into it, and then, by looking at that picture and going through the layers, the program is able to recognize that the image in that picture is that of a car.

If the program has been set up in the proper manner, it is going to make the right prediction that there is a car in the picture. The program is able to come up with this prediction based on some of the features that it already knows belongs to the car, including the color, the number on the license plate, the placement of the doors, the headlights, and more.

When you are working with some of the conventional coding methods that are available, this process can be really difficult to do. You will find that the neural network system can make this a really easy system to work with.

For the algorithm to work, you would need to provide the system with an image of the car. The neural network would then be able to look over the picture. It would start with the first layer, which would be the outside edges of the car. Then it would go through a number of other layers that help the neural network understand if there were any unique characteristics that are present in the picture that outlines that it is a car. If the program is good at doing the job, it is going to get better at finding some of the smallest details of the car, including things like its windows and even wheel patterns.

There could potentially be a lot of different layers that come with this one, but the more layers and details that the neural network can find, the more accurately it will be able to predict what kind of car is in front of it. If your neural network is accurate in identifying the car model, it is going to learn from this lesson. It will remember some of these patterns and characteristics that showed up in the car model and will store them for use later. The next time that they encounter the same kind of car model, they will be able to make a prediction pretty quickly.

When working with this algorithm, you are often going to choose one, and use it, when you want to go through a large amount of pictures and find some of the defining features that are inside of them. For example, there is often a big use for this kind of thing when you are working with face recognition software. All of the information wouldn't be available ahead of time with this method. And you can teach the computer how to recognize the right faces using this method instead. It is also one that is highly effective when you want it to recognize different animals, define the car models, and more.

There are a lot of advantages that come with using this kind of model for machine learning. One of these advantages is that you are going to be able to do this method without having to control the statistics of the algorithm. Even if you don't have the statistics available, or you don't know how to use them, you will find that the neural networks can be used to ensure that any complex relationship that is there is going to show up. This is true between both the variables that are independent and dependent, and even if these variables are nonlinear.

This isn't the perfect method to work with all of the time though. One of the biggest issues of the neural networks, and why you wouldn't want to use it all of the time, is that the cost of computing it can be high. For some businesses, and for some of the projects you would like to work on, this is just going to cost too much computational power, too much money, and too much time in order to get the work done.

Chapter 10: How the Random Forest Algorithm Can Help in Machine Learning

The decision tree and the random forest can often work together to help you get the results that you want with your algorithms. We will first take a look at decisions trees to see what they are about, and then move on to what the random forest is and how it compares with the decision tree.

The decision tree can be an efficient data tool if you want to be able to look at more than one choice, and these choices are very different, and then use the information that you gather in order to pick the right decisions out of those choices to help you to improve and grow your business.

When the various options are presented to you, you can use the decision tree in order to see all of the outcomes that each will provide to you. This helps you to see which decisions are the best to make, and can make it easier to come up with the predictions that you need to see success.

There are a few ways that you are able to work with the decision trees. Many of those in machine learning like to use it either for variables that are categorical, or the ones that are random. However, in many cases, machine learning is going to ask you to use these decision trees to help with any classification problem. To ensure that you are coming up with a good decision tree, you will need to take up all of the data sets that you are working on and then splitting them up into two or more sets, with similar data in each set. These can then be sorted out with the help of the independent variables because this is going to distinguish them out from the different sets.

So, that brings up the question that this seems hard to make work. In order to make sure that this is all going to work well, you will need to take a look at an example, Start out this exercise with the idea that there are 60 people in the class. All of these students will have three variables that are independent. These variables are going to include their class, their gender, and their heights. When you take a look at the students who are in the class, you will know before you start that there are 30 o them that like to spend their time play soccer.

Going from this information about which students like to play soccer, you decide that you want to create your own model so that you can figure out which half of the students in that class like to spend some time playing soccer, and which half of the students in the class don't spend their time playing soccer.

To figure out how to create the model that you want, your decision tree will need to take a look at all of the students that you have presented, and then divide them up into the right groups. The variables that you would use here would include the class, height, and gender from before. The hope is that when you are all done, you are able to present a homogenous set of students who enjoy doing the same things.

There are a few other algorithms that can work well when you are using a decision tree, and they are going to help you to split up the data that you have. This is going to give you a few subsets that you can work with, and they will produce good outcomes that are the most homogenous and help you to make the best decisions for your needs. Remember that you can have more if the situation calls for it. But in this example, we just need to work with two groups; one which consists of the students who play soccer, and one that consists of those who don't.

You will find that there are many times that you need to go through some complex data and the decision tree can help you to sort things out based on similarities and differences. These decision trees will provide you with a lot of the data that you need, and you can then take that data and make smart and informed decisions for the business.

Sure, you can use your intuition and some of the old and traditional forms of decision making. But you will find that the decision tree is going to make sure that this is much easier. The decision tree can help to get that information sorted through quickly, and may even show you much more information than you would be able to get with other methods, especially compared to having an employee use valuable time and resources to try and do the same thing.

The random forest

There are some times when the decision tree is not going to be the right choice for you when picking out algorithms that you want to use. When this happens, you may want to take some time to work with the algorithm that is known as a random forest. These random forests can be popular to work with, so if you plan to use machine learning on a regular basis, or you want to get more into the field of data science, then they are definitely a topic that you need to learn a bit more about.

Since these random forests are so well-known and popular, it is not too hard to see that they have the potential to help out with a lot o problems. For example, if you are looking to work with tasks that explore through the data, like dealing with values that are missing, or treating some of the outliers for the information that you have, then the random forest is going to be the best algorithm to help you out.

There are a few chances in machine learning where you will be able to bring these random forests out. This is because the random forest is perfect for providing you with the results that you need. And often they can do a better job, or do the job completely, than what you see with other algorithms. Some of the ways that you are able to use these random forests and make sure that they work towards your advantage includes:

- When you are working on your own training sets, you will find that all of the objects that are inside a set will be generated randomly, and it can be replaced if your random tree things that this is necessary and better for your needs.

- If there are M input variable amounts, then m<M is going to be specified from the beginning, and it will be held as a constant. The reason that this is so important because it means that each tree that you have is randomly picked from their own variable using M.

- The goal of each of your random trees will be to find the split that is the best for the variable m.

- As the tree grows, all of these trees are going to keep getting as big as they possibly can. Remember that these random trees are not going to prune themselves.

- The forest that is created from a random tree can be great because it is much better at predicting certain outcomes. It is able to do this for you because it will take all prediction from each of the trees that you create and then will be able to select the average for regression or the consensus that you get during classification.

Random forests are going to be a great tool for you to use when you want to bring out some data science with your machine learning, and there are a ton of advantages to working with the random forests rather than picking out some of the other algorithms that are out there. The first benefit is that the random forest is able to deal with both kinds of problems, whether they are regression or classification problems. Most of the other algorithms that you will work with only help with one or the other, rather than both of these problems.

Another benefit is that these random forests are going to be perfect when it is time to handle the larger amounts of data that you need to deal with, and you are able to add in thousands, and even hundreds of thousands of variables, to this kind of algorithm, and it is going to handle the information and give you the answers that you need. Of course, it isn't likely that you will send in that many variables to the system. But it is nice to know that there is enough power behind it that you have the potential to do this.

Before you decide to work with random forests though, you should remember that while they are able to work with the regression problems that show up in machine learning, they are not going to make any kinds of predictions that go past the training data you put in, or the ranges that are there.

This means that the random forests are going to help you make some predictions, and they will be able to help you come up with some of the best business decisions ever. But there are still going to be some limitations because it won't go past the ranges that you are able to provide to the algorithm, and this means that the accuracy that you have is going to be lower.

Chapter 11: How Can I Use TensorFlow

Now that we have spent some time taking a look at Scikit-learn and how that library works well, it is time to move into working with TensorFlow a little bit to get it to work well. To understand these tensors well, it is a good idea to first know a bit more about vector calculus and linear algebra. Tensors are going to be added into the TensorFlow as a multidimensional data arrays, but some more introduction will be needed in this part to ensure that you are able to really understand what tensors are about, and how they come to importance when you are doing machine learning.

Plane vectors

First, we need to know vectors. Vectors are going to be a special matrix type, ones that are going to contain rectangular arrays of numbers for machine learning. Because vectors are ordered collections of numbers, they will be seen in the view of column matrices. They will usually have just one column, along with however many rows that you need to see the results. In other words, you can think about the vectors as scalar magnitudes that have been given a direction.

Remember, a good example of scalar is 5 meters or 60 m/sec while a vector would be something like 5 meters north or 60 m/sec east. The difference between these two is going to be that the vector has a direction while the scalar doesn't. Despite this, these examples are still going to be different than what you are going to see when you start with some of the machine learning problems along the way. This is pretty normal. The length of the mathematical vector is going to be a pure number, meaning that it is absolute.

But, the direction that you work with is going to be relative. This direction is going to be measured out relative to some reference direction, and it is going to be shown in either degrees or units of radians. For the most part, you are going to need to assume that the direction is positive, and that it goes in a rotation that is counterclockwise from the direction that you used for reference.

When looking visually though, you will need to represent the vectors as arrows. This means that you will be able to consider these vectors as arrows that come with a length and direction. The direction that you will need to follow can be indicated by the head of the arrow, but then the length is going to be indicated by how long the arrow is.

So, this brings up the idea of what plane vectors are all about? Plane vectors are going to be a very straightforward setup of these tensors. They are going to be very similar to the regular vectors that we talked about before, with the sole difference being that they will find themselves in what is known as the vector space.

To get a better idea of what this means, let's take a look at an example of this. Let's say that you have a vector that goes 2 X 1. What this means is that the vector is going to belong to a set of real numbers that are paired two at a time. To say this in a different manner, they are going to both be a part of wo-space. When this occurs, you will be able to represent vectors on the coordinate (working with the idea of x, y) plane with the rays or the arrows.

Working from this coordinate plane going from the standard positions with the vectors having an endpoint at the origin (or at 0, 0), you will be able to derive the value of the x coordinate by looking at the first row of the vector. You could also find the y coordinate in the second row. Keep in mind that this standard position doesn't always need to stay the same or be maintained. The vectors are able to move parallel to themselves in the plane, without having to deal with any changes.

One thing to note here is that for vectors that are 3 by 1, you will talk about what is a three space. You will be able to show the vector in a three-dimensional figure with arrows pointing to positions in the vectors pace; they are going to be drawn on this with the standard x, y, and z axes.

It is a nice thing to have these vectors, and it is nice to represent them on the coordinate plane.

But in essence, you will have these vectors in place so that you are able to perform operations on them, and one thing that can help you in doing this is to express the vectors as either unit vectors or bases.

The unit vectors are going to be the ones that have magnitudes of one. You will often be able to recognize when you are looking at a unit vector when it has a lowercase letter with the circumflex or hat. Unit vectors are going to be very convenient to use if you want to make sure that your 2D or 3D vector is shown as a two or three orthogonal components.

Any time that you want to express one of the vectors as the sum of the component, you will see that we are actually talking about the component vectors, which will end up being two or more vectors whose sum that is given vector.

Getting started with the basics of TensorFlow

Since we have spent some time talking about the vectors and some of the things that you will need to know to get started here, you will now need to take some time to learn how to get TensorFlow all set up and ready to use some of the basics. We already talked how to install TensorFlow in an earlier chapter, so now it is time to take a look at how to actually work with this program.

You are generally going to write with TensorFlow programs, which you will run as a chunk. This is, when you look at it first, kind of contradictory, when you want to write out your programs in Python. However, if you are able to, or if you find it a bit easier, you can choose to work with TensorFlow's Interaction Session, which you can use to work more interactively within this same library. This can even be helpful when you want to work with IPython.

For what we are going to talk about in this section, we will want to put our focus on using the second option. This is going to help you to get a nice start with using the process of deep learning in TensorFlow. But before we get into some of the hard stuff and all the cool things that you are able to do with TensorFlow, we need to start out with some of the basic stuff to make it easier.

To do any of the basics, we need to first import the tensorflow library under the alias of “tf”, as we did before. We will then be able to initialize two variables that are going to be constants. Then you need to pass an array of four numbers using the function of “constant()”.

It is possible that you could go through and pass in an integer if you would like. But for the most part, working with and trying to pass an array is going to be easier and will work the best for your needs. Tensors are often about arrays so this is why it is better to use them.

Once you have put in the integer, or more likely the array, that you want to use, it is time to use the function of "multiply()" to get the variables to multiply together. Store the result as the "result" variable. And last, print out the result using the function of print().

Keep in mind that if you have defined the constants in the DataCampLight code. However, there are a few other value types that you can work with in this, namely known as the placeholders. These placeholders are important because they are going to be values that are unassigned and that can be initialized by the session where you choose to let it run. Like the name is giving away, the placeholder for a particular tensor that you want to work with will be fed when the session actually runs.

You can also work with variables. These are options that are going to have values that can change. The constants, though, are the values that you won't be able to change. If you want to make sure that no one can come in later on and make some changes to the values that you have in the equation, then you would want to work with the constants. If the fact that the values can change on occasion isn't that big of a deal to you, or you want the ability for the value to be changed, then you can work more with variables.

The results of the code you find correct will end with an abstract tensor in the computational graph. However, even though it may seem a bit contradictory in the process, the results with this aren't going to be calculated. It is just going to go through and define the model, but there wasn't a process ran in order to calculate the result.

Belgian Traffic Signs

While there are many people in the world of machine learning who already know all about traffic and what it means, we are still going to take a moment to go over the observations that are included in this dataset to ensure that everyone is on the same page before we progress any further. In this section, we are going to make sure that we are up to speed with all of the knowledge about domains that are needed before we start.

To get started, we need to take a look at some anecdotes to go with this and to help us set up for the exercises that we are going to do as we progress through this guidebook. To start, take a look at the information below:

1. The traffic signs that are found in Belgium are often going to come in French and Dutch. This is some good information to know about, but for the kind of datasets that we are going to explore soon, it's not too important.

2. There are going to be six categories of traffic signs that show up in Belgium. These include designatory signs, signs that would relate to standing still or parking on the road, mandatory signs, prohibitory signs, priority signs, and warning signs.

3. On January 1, 2017, there were more than 30,000 of these traffic signs that the country decided to remove from the roads in Belgium. All of the signs that were removed were prohibitory signs that were related to speed.

4. Talking about the removal, the overwhelming presence of traffic signs has been a big discussion in Belgium, and also inside the rest of the European Union, for some time.

Now that we have been able to gather a bit of the background information that we need, it is time to download the right dataset. You will need to work with the set of data that is found here.

When you do all of this, you are going to get two files that are zip files, to show up. They will be listed next to the "Belgium TS for Classification, or for cropped images. If you are searching for them, you will find that they are called:

"BelgiumTSC_Training" and
"BelgumTSC_Testing."

One tip here is that if you have gone through the

work to download the files, or you are going to do the downloading after you finish the tutorial, you will need to take a moment to look at the folder structure of the data that has been downloaded. You are going to see that the testing, and the training data folders, will come in with 61 subfolders. Inside of these subfolders, there are going to be 62 different types of traffic signs, and they are all going to be needed for the purpose of classification while you are in this process. You will also find that there are some files that come with the extension of .ppm, which stands for Portable Pixmap Format.

If you notice that all of these things do show up in the folders that are there now, you have been successful in downloading the images of the traffic signs! Now, we need to take a few moments to import the data over to your own workspace. We are going to start with the lines of code that are going to show up below the UDF, or the user-defined function using the function "load_data():"

1. First, you need to take some time to set up the ROOT_PATH. This is an important path to work with because it is one that you had made the directory at when you were first training and testing out the data that you have.

2. You can no go through and add in the specific paths that you are going to choose, using the ROOT_PATH and the help of the join() function. You will then be able to go through and store these two paths, even though they are unique, in the train_data_directory and in the test_data_directory.

3. You will see that after this point, you will be able to call the load_data() unction and

then pass over the train_data_directory to it.

4. Now you need to work with the function of load_data(). This function is going to start off by gathering together all of the subdirectories that will be present in that directory that we moved over. It is able to do this with the help of list comprehension, which is a very natural method to construct lists. What this does is it basically wants you to double check I something is in the directory. And if that item is in there, then add it to the list. Remember that each of the subdirectories is going to represent a label.

5. Next we have to loop through the subdirectories. To make this happen, you will first need to initialize two lists, which are going to be images and labels. Next,

you will need to go through and gather up the paths that you will use with the subdirectories, and the file names that go with the images that are stored in these subdirectories. After, you are able to collect the data in the two lists to help with the function of append().

The statistics of traffic signs

With all of this data loaded in, it is time to inspect the data. You can start with a simple analysis with the help of the size and the ndim attributes and the images array. Note here that the labels and images variables are going to be list. This means that it may be necessary to go through and convert these variables with the np.array() to an array in your own workspace.

Note that the images[0] that you printed out, in fact, is going to be a single image, but it will be represented by arrays inside of arrays. This can sometimes seem a bit strange, but as we work more with the images inside of machine learning, or even with deep learning, you will find that it is pretty common to work with.

You may want to stop and take a look at the labels here, just to check it out, but there won't be a lot of surprises that show up here. These numbers should provide you with some good insights into how successful the import was, and the size that your data is. You should be able to tell pretty quickly whether things are going to be set up the way that you want.

One tip to try out here is that you can try to add in the following attributes to make sure that your arrays are able to get more information including the total consumed bytes, the length of one array elements in bytes, and any information that you need to know about memory layout; nbytes, item size, and flags. You can take some time to test this out as needed.

How to visualize the traffic signs

The previous work that we did to do some checks of the system will help you get a good idea of the data that you are planning to work with, but if you are working with a lot of data that consists of images, there are a few steps that you can take to look through the data through the idea of visualizing it. To do this, we are going to take a moment to look at some more of the random traffic signs that you are going to work with:

1. To start, you need to make sure that you have the matplotlib or pyplot package. They can come under the common alias of plt.

2. Next, you will need to come up with a list

that has four random numbers. These are important because they are going to be what you use to come up with the right traffic signs from your images array, the same one that you went through and inspected in the last section. For our needs, we are going to pick out the numbers of 300, 3650, 2250, and 4000.

3. Now we need to say that for every element in the length of that particular list, so from 0 to 4, you will need to create subplots without the axes. This is done so that you won't go running with all the focus that you have solely on the images. With these new subplots you will need to pull out that specific image from your array that goes with the number at index 1. So, for the first loop, we will pass 300 over to images[]. The second one would go to 2250, and so on. Then, before you

finish, you will need to make sure the right adjustments are done to the subplots to ensure that there is enough room and width that occurs between each one of them.

4. The last thing that we need to work on here is to show how the plot is using the function of show().

When you go through and bring these pictures up in a loop, you will notice that the pictures don't come out in the same size! You can always mess around with these numbers and follow up a bit more if you choose, but the observations are often going to need to occur at the beginning of the process, and they need to happen when you start working more towards manipulating the data so that you can feed it over to the neural network.

How to use deep learning with TensorFlow

Now that we have looked a bit more at how to manipulate the data that you are working with, it is time to construct the neural network architecture, but we are going to help of the TensorFlow package.

Just like what you can do with the help of Keras, it's time to build up the neural network, going through this layer by layer. If you haven't taken the time to do it yet, make sure that you have gone through and imported the "tensorflow" into the workspace using the conventional alias of "tf" or another name as we need. Then, you will want to initialize the graph using the function of Graph() to help. You will need to use this function to help you define the computation.

Remember here that when you are working with

a graph, you won't need to take the time to compute anything. This is because the graph doesn't hold onto any values. It is just going to define the operations that you would like to have up and running for later.

In this case, we want to use the function of as_default() to help us get the right default context set up. This is going to work because it returns a context manager that makes the specific graph the default graph. You can use this method any time that you would like to create more than one graph in the same process. When you use the function that is above, you are going to come up with a global default graph where you are able to add all of your operations, unless you take the time to create a new graph.

Next, we need to take some time to add in the operations that we want to have in the graph. You will do this by building your model up, and then compiling it, and then you define the metric, the optimizer, and the loss function. You will be able to work with TensorFlow, you will be able to happen in one step. The things that you need to do for this includes:

1. Define the placeholders that you want to use for your labels and inputs, because we are not going to put in the real data at this time. remember that the placeholders that you are using here are values that are unassigned and that will be initialized as soon you as go through and run it. so, when you are ready to run the session, these placeholders are going to get the values from your set of data that you pass through in the function for run().

2. Now we want to work to build up our network. You can start this by flattening out the input, and this is done by working

with the function flatten(). This will give you an array of shape, rather than the shape that is used with images that are grayscale.

3. After you have been able to flatten up the input, your construct needs to become a fully connected layer that generates logits of size. Logits is going to be the function that operates on the unscaled output of previous layers. And then it is going to use the relative scale to make sure that there is an understanding that the units are linear.

4. After you have had some time to work with the perceptron that is multi-layer, you will then be able to make sure that the loss function is defined. The choice that you make with your loss function is going to depend on what kind of task you are

doing at the time.

a. Remember here that when you use regression, it is going to be able to predict values that are continuous. When you work with classification, you are going to predict the discrete classes or values of data points.

b. From here, you can wrap up the reduce_mean) function, which is going to compute out the mean of elements across the whole tensor.

5. Now you want to take the training optimizer and define that. Some of the best algorithms that you can use to optimize this include RMSprop, ADAM, and Stochastic Gradient Descent. Depending on the algorithm you use, you

may need to set up some time parameters, such as learning rate or momentum.

6. And to finish, you will need to initialize the operations in order to execute the whole thing before you go and start on the training.

These are just a few of the different things that you can work on when it comes to working with TensorFlow. This is a great program that you are able to work with in order to do some of the different things that you must work with machine learning. There is so much that you can do when you get started with machine learning, and you will find that working with TensorFlow can help you to get a lot of the work done.

Chapter 12: Working with Recurrent Neural Networks

When we are looking at the human brain, it is reasonable to understand that we don't restart our thinking from nothing each second. You will keep building up on what you have learned in the past, whether it is from your childhood, or from something that you learned a few seconds ago. As you read through the different parts of this guidebook, you will understand each of the words, based on how much understanding you had of the words that were there before. You won't just see a word and then throw it away, and then start over with your thinking from the beginning. It basically shows that your thoughts have some persistence and consistency with them.

A traditional neural network on machine learning isn't able to do this. And this can prove to be a big shortcoming in many cases. For example, if you want to take the time to classify the kind of event that is happening at each point of the movie, it is really hard to figure out how some of the traditional neural network could use its reasoning about events that happened earlier in the film in order to inform what happens later on.

The good news is that these recurrent neural networks that we are going to take a look at here are able to address this kind of issue in machine learning. They are networks that have some loops in them, which allows the information to persist. In this method, a loop is going to allow information to be passed from one part of the network will move over to the next. A recurrent neural network can be the similar idea as having multiple copies of the same network, with each message over to the successor.

This chain like nature is going to reveal that recurrent neural networks are going to be intimately related to lists and sequences. They are the natural architecture of a neural network to use for such data. And they will be used quite a bit. In the past few years, there is going to be a lot of success when you apply these to a variety of machine learning problems including image captioning, translation, language modeling, and speech recognition.

One of the glaring limitations that come with the vanilla neural networks is that their API is going to have a lot of constraints on it. They are only able to accept a fixed sized vector as their input, and then they can only produce a fixed sized vector as the output. But this is just one of the problems. These models are going to perform this mapping with a fixed amount of computational steps, which equals the number of layers that you will be able to see in the model.

The main reason that these recurrent options are going to add some more excitement into what you can do is because they allow the programmer to operate their work over a sequence of vectors. This includes sequences in the input, the output, and usually with both.

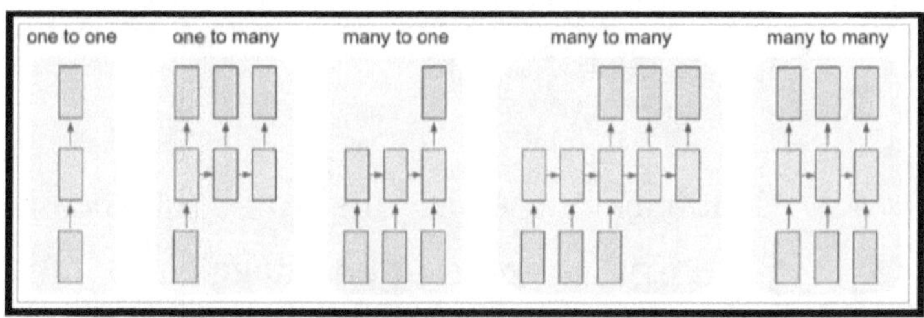

Let's take a look at the chart above. Each of the

rectangles that are there are going to be a vector and the arrows are going to show us the functions. The input vectors are going to show up in red, and then the output vectors that we need to know are going to be in blue. And then the green vectors will hold onto the RNN state (which we are going to talk about in a minute). Going freom the left over to the right, let's take a look at how each of these work:

1. The first one is going to be the vanilla mode of processing, the one that doesn't use the RNN at all. This is going to include an input that is fixed, and an output that is fixed. This is also known as image classification.

2. Sequence output is going to be the second part. This is going to be image captioning that is able to take an image and then will provide you with an output of a sentence of words.

3. Sequence input: This is goi going to be the third picture above. It is going to be more of a sentiment analysis that shows us a given sentence and makes sure that it is classified as either a negative or positive sentiment.

4. Sequence output and sequence output. You can find this one in the fourth box, and it is getting a bit closser to what we want. This one is going to be similar to a machine translation. This is when the RNN is able to read a sentence out in English, and then can take that inormation and provide you with an output that reads the sentence in rench.

5. And finally, the last box is going to be the synced sequence input and output. The video classification here is going to help us to label out each of the frames that occur in a video if we decide to.

Notice that in each of these, there aren't going to be any constraints put on the lengths of the sequences that we have to specify ahead of time. this is because the recurrent transformation, which is going to be shown in green, is fixed, and we are able to apply it out as many times as we would like, or as many times as work with our project.

An example of using RNN

In this example, we are going to take some time to train the RNN character level language mode. What this means is that we are going to give the RNN a big amount of text, and then we are going to ask it to model the probabilty of distribution of the next character in the sequence, given a sequence of previous characters. This is a good thing to work on because it ensures that we are able to generate some new text, going with just one character at a time.

As an example, suppose that we had a really limited vocabulary to work with, and just four possible letters, of helo. With this information, we want to train the RNN to do a training sequence of "hello" instead. This training sequence is going to be a source of four separate training examples This may sound a bit complex when we are first getting started, but we will take this step by step to help you see how it works. Some of the things to cnsider to get this started includes:

1. The probability of getting "e" should be just as likely to occur as getting the letter "h".

2. "L should be likley in the context of "he"

3. The "l" should also be likely if the system is given the context of "hel"

4. "o" should be likely if the other sequences have happened and the context of "hell" is in place.

Now we are going to encode each of the characters that occur in the vector working with the 1 of k incoding (this is going to ean that we will use all zeroes except for a single one at the index of the character in the vocabulary). We will then be able to feed them into the RNN, doing so one at a time, using the function for step to make this happen.

Once all of this has gottne into place, we are going to observe a sequence of 4-dimensional output vectors, with one dimension showing up for each character, which we can then interprest as the confidence that the RNN is able to assign right now to each of the characters that come up in the next seqnece at a time. Let's take a look at a diagram that can show up when it is time to run this kind of sequence.

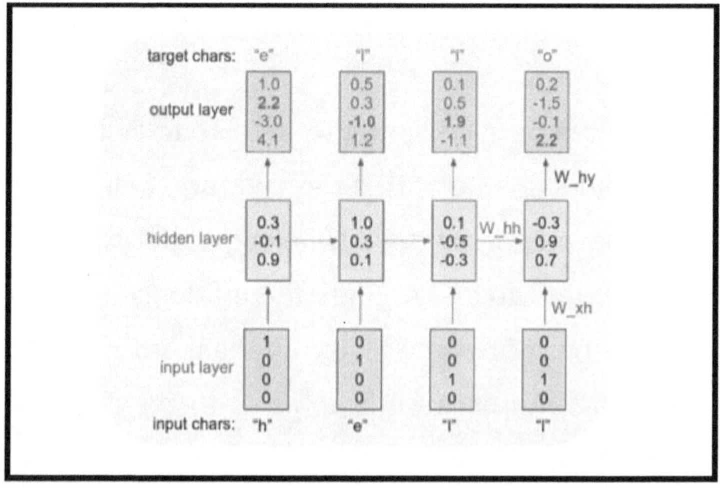

Out of this, we may use an example of seeing that in the first time step, the RNN would see the character of "h" it was able to assign some confidence to this of 1.0, to the next letter turning into "h", 2.2 to getting the letter "e" -3.0 to "l" "and 4.1 to "o". Since the training data that we are using, (which is the string of hello that we talked about above), had the next right character being "e" we want to increase the confidence, or the green color, and then decrease how confident it is in all of the other letters, which are going to be shown in the red above.

In addition, we are going to need to take another step and come up with a desired target character at every one of the four time steps that we want the network to assign a great confidence to. This takes a bit more time to accomplish, but it can be really helpful because it helps us to get the right amount of confidence that the system is able to assign the right letters at the right time.

Since we are working with RNN and it is going to consist entirely of the differentiable operations, we are able to use the back-propagation algorithm. What this is includes a recursive application of the chain rule from calculus. We are able to use this in order to figure out what direction we are able to adjust all of the weights in order to ensure that we have been able to increase the scores of the correct targets, which are going to be the green and bold numbers.

Once we have been able to do this, we are able to work on what is known as a parameter update. This is going to nudge all the weights a tiny amount into the direction that we want. If we are able to make sure that the inputs we feed into the RNN are the same after each of the updates of the parameter, we will find that the scores of the correct characters, would end up being a big higher (meaning it would go from a 2.2 up to a 2.4) and that the incorrect characters would go down a little bit.

Now, you may need to go through and repeat this process over and over again quite a few times in order to make it work. The number of times that this has to happen is going to depend on how complex the system is. since we are working with a simple word of hello here, you probably won't have to do it too much. But since machine learning is going to be a big programming technique and it can get complicated, it is possible that you will need to do this many times. You will want to repeat the process until you are able to get the network to converge, and you are able to get the predictions to be consistent with the training data in that the correct characters are always predicted in the same order, and the correct order, each time that you are able to run the program.

We can also work with an explanation that is a bit more technical here. And we are able to do this once we work with the standard Softmax classifier, which is sometimes referred to as the cross entropy loss) on every output vector at the same time. you will be able to train the RNN with the mini-batch Stochastic Gradient Descent, and you may find that working with Adam or RMSProp to make sure that the updates are as stable as possible.

When you do all of this, you should notice that the first time that the character of “l” is inputted to this, the target is “l” but the second time the target is going to be “o”. The RNN is not going to be able to just rely on the input on its own, and it is going to need to bring in some recurrent connection to help keep track of the context that is needed to make this task achievable.

When you get to testing time, you will be able to go in and feed the right characters into the RNN algorithm. And once that is put in, you should be able to see the distribution over what characters the system is going to bring out next, and see if you get the answers that you want. We will then be able to sample from the distribution that we are given, and then we feed it all right back in to see which letter you are going to get next. You can then just repeat this process until you get everything in the right order, and you will find that you are sampling the text.

As you can see here, there are a lot of different things that you are able to do with the RNN algorithm that just aren't possible when you are working with the other options out there. it opens up a lot more doors, and ensures that you can handle a lot more situations in the process.

Chapter 13: Linear Classifier

As you are working some more with supervised learning, you may find that two of the most common tasks that you will have to spend time with include the linear classifier and the linear regression. The linear regression is going to predict the value, and then the linear classifier will focus on the class. For this chapter, we are going to take a look more at the linear classifier and how it can be used to help you with machine learning.

You will quickly find that when you are doing machine learning, these classification problems are going to take up at least 80 percent of the machine learning tasks that you need to do. The classification aims at predicting how probable it is for each class to occur given the set of inputs that you add in. the label, which is going to be the dependent variable in this case, is going to be known as a discrete value, and is called a class. If your label, or dependent variable, has only two classes to work with, then you will know that your learning algorithm is a binary classifier. If you are working with a classifier that is more multiclass, this means that it is going to tackle the labels that have more than two classes.

For example, many of the classification problems that are binary are going to predict the likelihood that your customer is going to come back and make a second purchase. But if you would like the system to make a prediction about the type of animal that is shown on a picture, you will then be working with a multiclass classification problem because there are going to be more than two varieties of animals that are in the picture.

How can I measure the performance of a linear classifier?

The first thing that we need to take a look at is the linear classifier. Accuracy is a good place to start. The performance overall of the classifier is measured with the accuracy metric. Accuracy is able to collect all of the right values that you have, and then it divides it by the total number of observations that are present. For example, if you have a value of accuracy that ends up being 85 percent, this means that when your model is put to use, it is going to be correct 85 percent of the time, and incorrect 15 percent. Your goal is to get the percentage correct up to as high as possible.

As you are looking at this, you may be able to note that there is a shortcoming that will happen in this metric, especially if you are looking at a class of imbalance. A data set that is imbalanced can occur when the amount of observations that show up is not going to be equal in each group.

So, let's say that you are trying to do a classification of a rare event with your function of logistics. You may imagine that the classifier that you use is going to try and estimate how many patients died when they got a particular disease. In the data, five percent of your patients who get this disease are going to pass away. With this idea, you are able to train your classifier to make sure that it is able to make a good prediction of the number of deaths that do occur, and then you can work with the metric of accuracy to evaluate the performances of that hospital or clinic. Now, if the classifier goes to work and predicts that there are 0 death for the whole set of data, then it is going to be correct about 95 percent of the time here.

Next, we need to take a look at what is known as

the confusion matrix. This is actually a better way to take a look at the performance of the classifier compared to the accuracy. When you are working with the confusion matrix, you will be able to visualize how accurate the classifier is by comparing the actual and the predicted classes. Your binary confusion matrix is going to be made up of squares. The parts that you will see in this kind of matrix is as follows:

1. TP: This is going to known as the true positive. This is going to contain all of the predicted values that were correctly predicted as an actual positive.

2. FP: This is going to be the false ones, or the ones that were predicted in an incorrect manner. They were usually predicted as positive, but they were actually negative. This means that the negative values show up, but they had

been predicted ahead of time as positive.

3. FN: This is false negative. This is when your positive values were predicted as negative.

4. TN: this is going to be the true negative. These are the values that were predicted in a correct manner and were predicted as actual negative.

When you take a look at one of these of these confusion matrix, you will be able to see a clear look at the actual class and the predicted class and see what is going on there.

Looking at precision and sensitivity

You are going to get a lot of great information that comes from the confusion matrix. It is able to provide you with some good insight into the false positive and the true positive. But, there are some cases where it is preferable to have a metric that is more concise.

First we need to take some time to look at the precision. The precision metric is going to show us the accuracy of the positive class. This basically means that it is going to give us a good idea and a good measure of how likely the prediction of the positive class is going to be correct. The formula that you can use to figure out what the precision is includes:

Precision = TP/(TP + FP)

The maximum score that you can get here is one. And this is going to show up the classifier perfectly comes up correctly with the positive values. Precision alone is not going to be that helpful because it is going to ignore the negative class. This metric is something that you may want to pair up with the recall metric. The recall is also called sensitivity or true positive rate.

The next thing that we need to take a look at is the sensitivity. This sensitivity is important because it is going to help us compute the ratio of positive classes that the algorithm was able to detect correctly. This metric can be a good way to model and take a look at a positive class. The formula for figuring out the sensitivity is:

Recall = TP/(TP + FN)

How linear classifiers work with TensorFlow?

We spent some time earlier in this guidebook taking a look at TensorFlow and what it is all about. Now it is time to take it into some more practical work and look at how linear classifiers are able to work with this program. We are going to do this with the help of the census data set. The purpose of doing this is to make sure that we use the variables in the census data set in order to help is predict the level of income of our participants. Note that the income in this one is going to be a binary variable.

We will have our binary variable be at one if the income of the individual is greater than $50,000. But if the income is less than this amount, we will have the binary variable come out as 0. The data set that we are going to work with here will come with eight categorical variables that include:

Native country
Sex
Race
Relationship
Occupation
Marital status

Education

And place of work

And on top of this, we are going to take a look in this at six of the continuous variables. These are going to include:

Hours_week

Capital_loss

Capital_gain

Education_num

Fnlwgt

Age

From there, you will be able to work with TensorFlow in order to create a probability to see which individuals or customers are going to fit into each group. They will be separated out into the two groups initially, those who make over $50,000 and those who make under that amount. But you will be able to take a look into each group then and figure out some of their background information, where they live, their race and sex, and what they do for work and so much more. This is a tool that many businesses could start to rely on because they will get a better idea of what their repeat customers look like, and can better market to these individuals.

Generative models vs. discriminative models

When you are working on the parameters of the linear classifier, there are going to be two methods or classes, which are pretty broad, that can help you to figure out how to determine these parameters. They can either be a discriminative model or a generative model. Methods of the generative model are going to be conditional density function. The two biggest examples of these algorithm are going to include the Linear Discriminant Analysis, which will assume the Gaussian conditional density models, or the Naïve Bayes classifier.

The second method that you can work with is going to be the discriminative model. These are important because they are going to work in order to make sure that the output you have is as high quality as possible when you do a training set. Additional terms in the training may be necessary, but they can cost more and could easily perform the regularization of the final model. Some of the different options of discriminative training includes:

1. Logistic regression. This is going to be the likelihood estimation of linear classifiers assuming that the observed training set was generated by a binomial model that depends on the output of the classifier.

2. Perceptron: This is a type of algorithm

that you are going to use because it will try to go through and fix up any and all of the errors that can occur in a training set.

3. Support vector machine: This is one of the options that we talked about before. It is going to be the algorithm that will be able to maximize, as much as possible, the margin that can come between the examples that re in the training set and the decision hyperplane.

Despite the look of the name there, the LDA is not going to belong to the discriminative models in this method. However, the name does make sense when you are able to compare it to some of the other algorithms that are there, such as with principal components analysis. You will find that the LDA algorithm is going to fit in with supervised learning and it is going to be able to utilize the labels on your data, but the PCA is going to be an algorithm of unsupervised learning, and it purposely goes through and ignores the labels that are present.

You will find that with discriminative training, you are going to get a lot higher accuracy in place than working with conditional density functions. But, if you are working with the conditional density models, handling the data that may be missing is going to be a lot easier, so keep that in mind while doing some of these options.

Chapter 14: Other Processes You Can Use with Python Machine Learning

In addition to some of the different algorithms that we have talked about so far in this guidebook that have to do with machine learning, there are a lot of other options that you can go with as well. These can be very valuable to learn depending on the projects that you would like to create or what information you wish to go through. This chapter is going to explore some more of the machine learning algorithms that you can work with to help you get the most out of your needs.

Naïve Bayes

The first method that we are going to take a look at is the Naïve Bayes. To understand how this one is going to work, we may need to use a bit of imagination. To do this, you can imagine that you are working on a project that can include classification problems, but you want to make sure that you are able to come up with a new hypothesis that actually works, and you want to also come up with a design that allows you to have a new feature and discussion based on how important each variable has.

While this may seem like a lot of work, and like we are trying to do a lot in a short amount of time, but it can be done. Once you take some time to collect all of the information, it is likely that you will have a few stakeholders in your company who will show some interest in looking at a model of what you would like to produce. They may even want to see it a long time before the work is done. This can present a dilemma. You want to make sure that you are presenting this in a way that makes sense, but if the work is not all the way done, it can be hard to do this.

In many cases, when you are working with your data, you will have thousands of data points, or more, that you would like to show on your model. There an even be some new variables that will come up when you are doing all of your testing and training. How is it possible for you to show off this information to your shareholders in a way that they can understand and that actually shows the information that you want?

The good news is that there is an algorithm that you can work with that will help you to stick with an early stage of the model that is easy to understand while you can still show all of the information that is needed. The algorithm that you will use for this is called the Naïve Bayes algorithm and it is a great way to use a few demonstrations to showcase your model, even when it is still at an earlier stage of development.

Let's take a look at how this is going to work with an example of apples. When you grab what is considered an average apple, you will easily be able to state that there are some distinguishing features that are present. This could include the fact that the apple is red, that it is round, and that it will be around three inches round. While these can sometimes be found in some other types of fruits, when all of these features are present together, then we know that the fruit in our hands is an apple. This is a basic way of thinking, but this is an example of working with the Naïve Bayes.

The Naïve Bayes model is meant to be easy for you to put together, and it is sometimes used to help you get through really large sets of data in a way that is simplified. One of the advantages of working with this model is that though it is simple, it is sometimes better to work with compared to the other, more sophisticated models that you can work with.

As you learn more about how to work with this algorithm, you will start to find that there are more and more reasons for you to work with it. This model is really easy to use, especially if you are a beginner to the world of deep learning and machine learning. You will also find that it can be really effective when it is time to make some predictions for our data sets and what class they should end up in. This makes it easier for you to keep things as simple as possible during the whole process. Even though the Naïve Bayes algorithm is really simple to work with, you will find that it is able to perform really well. In fact, when compared to some of the higher-class algorithms that are out there, and some of the ones that seem to be more sophisticated, this one is going to perform the best.

However, even though there are a lot of benefits

that come with the Naïve Bayes method, you need to be careful because there are a few negatives that come with it. The first negative is that when you work with an algorithm that is set with categorical variables, you need to make sure that the data you are testing hasn't already gone through a data set for training. You may find that this algorithm is going to run into some issues when it comes to making accurate predictions, and often the data sets that it assigns information to will be based more on probability than anything else.

While there are some options to help out with this, and can ensure that you are able to solve the issue, it can sometimes be confusing to do this if you are a beginner and have never been able to work with machine learning. Of course, while Naïve Bayes is a great option for machine learning, it isn't going to be the only one that you need. But, if you do come prepared with all of the information that you need to plot, and you want to be able to showcase the information in a manner that is simplified to your shareholders, even if the model isn't done, then working with this algorithm is going to be a great choice to go with.

Regression algorithm

The next algorithm that you can consider is known as the regression analysis. This is the type that you will want to look into when you want to see if there is a relationship, and what type of relationship, that is able to show up between the dependent variables and the predictor variables. You will see that this technique is going to work well when you are looking to check out whether there is a casual relationship between the forecasting, the variable you are working with, or the time-series modeling in place. The point of the regression algorithm in machine learning is that it is going to help take all of your information and fit it onto a line, or a simple curve, as much as you can. This may not always happen depending on the data points that you are working with, but it can work well to help you see if there are any kinds of factors in common with the data points that will be seen on a graph.

There are many companies who will use the regression algorithm in order to help them make great predictions that will increase their profits. You will be able to use it in order to come up with a great estimation of the sales growth for the company while still basing it on how the economic conditions in the market are doing right at this moment.

The great thing about this is that you are able to add in any information that you would like to use. You can add in information about the past and the current economy to this particular algorithm, such as your past and current economic information, and then this gives you an idea of how the growth is going to go in the future. Of course, you do need to have the right information about the company to make this happen.

For example, if you use the regression algorithm and find that your company is growing at the same rate as what other industries are doing in the economy, you would then be able to use this information to help make predictions for how your company will do in the future if the economy does end up changing.

You will find that there are a few variations that come with the regression algorithm and you will need to choose the one that you want based on the information that you are trying to get from the algorithm. Some of the most common regression algorithms that you may want to use with machine learning include:

- Linear regression
- Polynomial regression
- Logistic regression
- Ridge regression
- Stepwise regression

As you can see, working with the regression algorithms are going to have a few different benefits that come with them. To start, you will see that these algorithms make it easy for anyone using the information to see what relationship is present, if any, between the dependent variables and the independent variables. This algorithm is also able to show what kind of impact will happen if you try to add in a new variable or change up another kind of variable that is in your data set.

Even though there are several benefits with this method, there are a few things to be away of when working on the regression algorithm. The biggest shortcoming that you will quickly notice is that you aren't able to use this algorithm to help out with any classification problem that comes up. The reason that classification problems and the regression algorithm don't always work together is because this particular algorithm tries to overfit the data many times. So, if you do try to add in different constraints here, you will find that the whole process is going to get tedious pretty quickly.

Clustering algorithms

While we did talk a bit about clustering earlier on in this guidebook, it is important to take a closer look at some of the options that are available, and how they can benefit you quite a bit. These clustering algorithms are often known as unsupervised machine learning algorithms, so you will be able to make sure that the algorithm and the program can learn things all on its own.

When we are taking a look at these clustering algorithms, it is important to make sure that things are as simple as you can make it. This method will take some of the data that you have and then make sure that clusters are going to come together. Before you start up the program at all, you get the benefit of picking out how many clusters you want to make all the information fit into. This is often going to depend on how much data that you want to put in, and what information you are hoping to get out of this thing.

For example, if you want to sort out the information between male and female customers, you would probably come up with two clusters. But if you want to figure out the age group of your customers, or some other thing with your data, you may want to have five or more clusters. The program, after you have input the number of clusters that you want to work with, and will take the data points and divide them up into which cluster they tend to do the best with.

The nice thing about this algorithm is that it is responsible for doing most of the work for you. This is because it is in charge of how many of your data points are going to fit into those clusters that you chose. To keep things organized, we are going to call all of your main clusters that you picked cluster centroids.

So, when you are looking at one of your clusters and you notice that there are a lot of points inside of it, you can safely make the assumption that all those particular data points have something in common or they are similar. There is some attribute or another that all the data points in one cluster have in common with each other.

Once these original clusters are formed, you can take each of the individual ones and divide them up to get more cluster sets if you would like. You can do this several times, creating more divisions as you go through the steps. In fact, you could potentially go through this enough times that the centroids will stop changing. This is when you know you are done with the process.

There are several reasons why you would want to work with a clustering algorithm to help you get a program started when doing machine learning. First, doing your computations with the help of a clustering algorithm can be easy and cost efficient, especially compared to some of the supervised learning options that we talked about before. If you would like to do a classification problem, the clustering algorithms are efficient at getting it done.

With that said, you do need to use some caution

here though. This algorithm is not going to be able to do the work of showing predictions for you. If you end up with centroids that are not categorized the right way, then you may end up with a project that is done the wrong way.

The Markov Algorithm

Another type of unsupervised machine learning algorithm that you can work with is the Markov algorithm. This particular algorithm is going to take the data that you decide to input into it, and then it will translate it to help work in another coding language if you choose. The nice thing here is that you can pick out which rules you want to use with this algorithm ahead of time so that the algorithm will work the way that you want. Many programmers in machine learning find that this algorithm, and the fact they can set up their own rules ahead of time, is nice because it allows you to take a string of data and ensure that it is as useful as possible as you learn on the job and figure out the parameters of how the data will behave.

Another thing that you may like about this Markov algorithm is that you are able to work with it in several ways, rather than being stuck with just one method. One option to consider here is that this algorithm works well with things like DNA. For example, you could take the DNA sequence of someone, and then use this algorithm to translate the information that is inside that sequence into some numerical values. This can often make it easier for programmers, doctors, and scientists and more to know what information is present, and to make better predictions into the future. When you are working with programmer and computers, you will find that the numerical data is going to be much easier to sort through than other options of looking through DNA.

A good reason why you would need to use the Markov algorithm is because it is great at learning problems when you already know the input you want to use, but you are not sure about the parameters. This algorithm is going to be able to find insights that are inside of the information. In some cases these insights are hidden and this makes it hard for the other algorithms we have discussed to find them.

There are still some downfalls to working with the Markov algorithm. This one can sometimes be difficult to work with because you do need to manually go through and create a new rule any time that you want to bring in a new programming language. If you only want to work with one type of programming language on your project, then this is not going to be a big deal. But many times your program will need to work with several different languages, and going in and making the new rules a bunch of times can get tedious.

Q-learning

Now it is time to take a look at some of the reinforced machine learning techniques. The first one that we will look at is known simply as Q-learning. With the Q-learning algorithm, you will find that it works the best with something called temporal difference learning. As you try to work with some of the different machine learning types, you may notice that this one is more of an off-policy algorithm because it does have the capability to learn an action value function. What this means is that you will get the results that you want and that you expect, no matter which state you are in.

Since you can take the Q-learning algorithm and use it no matter what function you need to create, you will need to take the time to go through this and list out any of the specifications that are needed for how the user or the learner will select the course of action. This is going to add in a few more steps to the process, but can be worth your time and effort.

After the programmer, which in this case is going to be you, goes through and finds the action value function that you are the most interested in using, it is time for you to work on creating the optimal policy. The best way to construct this is to use the actions that you think will come in at the highest value, no matter which of the states you choose to work with.

There are a number of advantages that you are going to find when working with the Q-learning algorithm. One of these that you will enjoy is that you won't have to take the time or the effort to put in the models of the environment for the system to compare it means. You can choose to compare a few, or many, actions together, and the type of environment that you use with this one won't really matter as much as with other methods.

SARSA

The second option that you can work with when it comes to reinforcement machine learning is known as the SARSA algorithm. The SARSA is going to be an acronym for state action reward state action algorithm. When you are working with this, you must take the time to describe the decision process policy that will occur in your Markov algorithm that we talked about earlier in this chapter.

This would then be the main function that you would use with the updated -value which will then rely on whatever the current state of the learner is. It can also include the reward that the learner is going to get for the selection they make, the action that the learner choose, and then the new state that the learner is going to be in when they are done with that action. As you can see, there are a ton of different parts that will end up coming together in order to make the SARSA work for your needs.

While there are many parts that most come together for this one, this is sometimes seen as the safest algorithm for a programmer to use when they are trying to find the solution they want to use. However, there can possibly be times when your learner is going to end up with a reward that is higher than what the average is for their trials. This is a bigger issue with the SARSA compared to some of the other algorithms that you have.

There are also going to be times when the learner ends up not going with the optimal path either.

Depending on how the program decides to react to this, it could bring up some issues with how they learn and how the program is going to behave for them.

As you can see, there are a lot of different algorithms that you can use when it comes to machine learning. These include a wide variety of supervised, unsupervised, and reinforcement learning to ensure that you get the results that you want, depending on the method or the program that you want to create.

Conclusion

The next step is to get started with some of the topics that we have discussed in this guidebook. There are so many cool things that you are able to do when you learn a little bit about machine learning. And when you combine together some of the aspects that you know of Python, even a beginner can create some really strong and powerful programs. This guidebook is meant to take you through some of the steps that you need to know, in order to be successful with python machine learning.

There are a lot of different things that you are able to do when machine learning is introduced. You can work on creating a recommendation guide to those who come and visit your website. You can set up a search engine on your page. You can even have the computer go through and work on a program that can go through large amounts of data and come up with the patterns and the information faster and more efficiently than you will see with any traditional programs.

What makes this even more incredible is the fact that, even though machine learning is so complex and can handle a ton of different situations with programming is that it can work with the Python coding language. Python is one of the best coding languages out there, as we explored in this guidebook, and it is going to be able to handle most of the programming needs that you have, while still being easy enough for a beginner to learn.

This guidebook took some time exploring the basics of both of these two technological programming tools, and how they are able to work together. We spent some time looking at the basics of the Python coding language, and then, when we moved back into the sphere of machine learning, we explored some of the ways to write codes, using the Python language, that made our machine learning really work great!

Machine learning is often seen as similar to artificial intelligence, and this is true. While there are some differences, machine learning is the technology that goes behind artificial intelligence, but that is just one of the many things that you are able to work with when it comes to machine learning. This guidebook took some time to explore these choices, and to help you understand the basics of putting this kind of programming and technology to work.

Adding the Python language to your machine learning projects can ensure that you get the power, speed, and the strength that you need in all of your codes. Sure, you can do these kinds of programming techniques with other languages, but none are as good as Python. And this guidebook will show you exactly how to put the two of them together for the best results.

When you are ready to make some amazing programs, and work with codes that are able to each themselves how to behave, make sure to check out this guidebook to help you get started!

www.ingramcontent.com/pod-product-compliance
Lightning Source LLC
LaVergne TN
LVHW091410190726
843491LV00006B/1365

9783903331310